MULTICULTURAL EDUCATION:
A Synopsis

H. Prentice Baptiste, Jr.
Professor of Education
Chairperson, Multicultural/Bilingual Education
College of Education
University of Houston
Houston, Texas

University Press
of America™

University Press of America, Inc.™

4710 Auth Place, S.E., Washington, D.C. 20023

All rights reserved
Printed in the United States of America

ISBN: 0-8191-0851-0
Library of Congress Number: 79-89924

371.97
B22 mJ

TABLE OF CONTENTS

Acknowledgements

Special appreciation is extended to my doctoral students at the University of Houston during 1973-79. Although I accept full responsibility for this final product, the essence of this booklet emanates from scholarly and motivationg interaction sessions with my doctoral students.

Although many individuals rendered support in the development of this revised edition, several individuals must be singled-out for their special contributions. Dr. Victoria Bergin, Houston Independent School District, wrote the bilingual section. Eileen Straus, doctoral student in Multicultural/ Bilingual Education, helped me with the revising and reviewing of the selected readings which appeared in the Mini-Reviews section. Dr. Thelma Cobb, Southern University, Baton Rouge, Louisiana, contributed to the writing of the section on Multicultural Education: An Evolving Concept in American Education.

Special thanks and appreciation is extended to Mira Lanier Baptiste, my wife, whose constructive criticisms, understanding and support played a major role in helping me bring this product to fruition.

Introduction

Acceptance of the concept of cultural pluralism in America has out-distanced its implementation in American education. Attempts to close the gap have been reflected in many discrete educational endeavors. The program emphases in these efforts have run the gamut from the disadvantaged, to minorities, to ethnic groups. Both the impetus and support of programs to implement these emphases grew largely out of legislative and judicial mandates to effectuate the changes occuring in the society. Each of these mandates, to some extent, specifically addressed the problem of education. Implicit in each decision was the need to reorder the priorities of the American educational system in terms of the ethnic cultural realities of the times.

Advocates of multicultural education view it as one of the more viable means for operationalizing the concept of cultural pluralism in the American educational system. Multicultural education recognizes the legitimacy of diversity and the contributions of diverse cultural groups. It encourages the comparative study of ethnic cultural groups to develop "literacy" not only about oneself but about others. It recognizes the importance of cultural diversity not only to education but to the society that education tends to reflect and the culture it transmits.

The selections provided in this volume are presented neither as an answer nor as a defense. Instead, they are reflections on relatively broad areas of multicultural considerations. The first selection views the evolution of multicultural education as a gradual progression in an educational system consistent with the prevailing national ethos: first, class consciousness, then racism, and finally cultural pluralism. The movement from a dual system to an integrated system would appear to follow this line of progression. In the second selection, some of the issues and problems associated with multicultural education are presented, together with proposed solutions. Stress is placed upon the need for more definitive research in the area and for the unification of discrete programs that seek a common goal. The third selection provides an overview of problems and issues related to bilingual education. Special emphasis is placed on the interrelatedness of language and culture and the need to understand the relationship in the planning of educational experiences.

The remaining selections should prove to be helpful to students of multicultural/bilingual education. There are brief reviews of several books of special interest, a selected bibliography, and a definitive glossary of basic concepts. The volume, as its title suggests, is a synopsis, but it should serve to initiate discussion, to encourage research, and to challenge those new to the area to broaden their knowledge base in the areas of culture and ethnicity. For, multicultural education may well be the vehicle by which American education becomes truly representative "of the people, for the people, by the people"—people of all ethnic cultural groups.

Multicultural Education: An Evolving Concept in American Education

Anyone who attempts to write about the evolution of any specific process in American education must be prepared to paint on a broad canvas in strokes not always clearly visible or understood by those who view his handiwork. His viewers or readers must also be prepared to accept as a point of departure certain propositions as basic with the full knowledge that the writer will insert many caveats before his work is finished. The end product will be an incomplete fusion of various colors interspersed with light and shade. For the evolution of education in America and the many philosophies, organizational schemes and approaches accompanying that evolution have been intricately bound up with the growing diversity of the population, the increasing complexity of the society, and the extension of educational opportunity to an increasingly diverse population.

There is not at this point a scholarly concensus as to a universally understood or accepted definition of multicultural education, but most statements that attempt to delineate its nature and purpose have as central tenets ethnic legitimacy and cultural diversity. That the American population has always reflected cultural diversity is not accepted as a given in the social and cultural history of America. The Native Americans met the colonists when they arrived. The Mexican, already representing two cultures, Spanish and Indian, came into the United States with the Southwestern and Western territories acquired from Mexico.[1] The English present everywhere, were dominant in New England and the South. The Scottish peopled much of the upland regions away from the coast; the Dutch were in New York; the Germans in Pennsylvania, the French Huguenots in South Carolina, a few Swedes in Delaware, and the black bondsmen of African descent were in a large measure ubiquitous. These ethnic entities were overlaid by a religious diversity that at times gave vent to old world antipathies. Such was the ethnocultural base out of which the American system of education emerged. The purpose of this chapter is to identify the antecedents of multicultural education and trace the development of the concept to its present status.

Providing a system of education to meet the needs of a culturally diverse population has been a recurring issue in American education. Two hundred years ago when the country was founded, the forefathers envisioned a nation oriented toward the welfare of its people. Life, liberty, and the pursuit of happiness were inalienable rights. To secure these rights, one of the major delivery systems was education. Education was considered necessary for the promotion of the moral, social, and economic development of the citizenry and the proper functioning of the new democratic system. The institution of a system of education, however, posed a problem. The crux of the problem, then as now, arose from the realization that the citizenry was a diverse group, in spite of its basically western European origins, and that this diversity encompassed class, caste, and ethnicity.

Efforts to solve the problem led to three distinct approaches: dual, plural, and multicultural. The first approach, based on class and later on race, lasted with legal sanction until the Brown Decision of 1954. This approach, geared to assimilation, recognized the existence of a single dominant cultural criterion, Anglo Saxon. The other two approaches recognized the importance of the Anglo Saxon ethos but also gave weight to the existence and impact of other cultures. Though both approaches are currently operative, the multicultural approach appears to be gaining the support of elements of the educational establishment whose advocacy protends the acceptance of this approach.

The issue of cultural diversity during the early period in the development of, the country was designated under a different rubric. That the question of culture, *vis-à-vis* education, was more implicit than explicit may be due to (a) the cultural hegemony of northern and western European backgrounds (b) inherited leanings toward European high culture (c) existing pedagogy had not clearly established a connection between culture and education, and (d) the concept of public education had not fully evolved.

Within these parameters, cultural diversity existed, its primary basis being social class. Consequently, the first phase of the dual education system emerged to meet the needs of two distinct social classes within the society. For the upper class, Latin grammar schools were designed to train scholars to give intellectual leadership in the church and other professions. For the lower class, elementary schools and apprenticeship systems were instituted to provide the rudiments of learning associated with religion and the development of useful skills.

Further, a dual system based on social class was consistent with the work ethic embraced by most of the settlers. From the vantage point of the upper class, the system did not "contribute to the growth of a poverty or vagabond class that would be a threat to the more stable elements of society."[2] For the lower class, the system appeared to help them feel that they were contributing, productive members of society and that the possibility existed for their achieving upward social and economic mobility. In addition to recognizable differences in social class, religious differences existed. With the exception of Catholicism, religious diver-

3

sity was treated as inter or intra group religious disagreement or differences. The major educational issue was the problem of religious vs. public control, instruction, and financing of education.

It might be noted that when an awareness of cultural diversity began to appear, it was reflected in issue oriented, not people oriented, concerns. Social class, the separation of church and state, and economic development dominated educational concerns. This attitude is plausible when one considers the fact that the population, generally, represented the Anglo Saxon Protestant ethos common in England, Germany, and Scandinavia, with persons from Ireland constituting a somewhat marginal group. The most visible "troublesome presence"[3] was the slave, whose education was not only declared illegal but believed to be impossible. Consequently, cultural diversity, as presently conceived, evoked little concern because the dominant group was representative of the established culture criterion. This belief was supported by the influential works of Spencer and others who placed European culture (especially northern and western European) at the top of the cultural hierarchy.[4] It was, in all probability, this belief that led in large measure to the creation of the Melting Pot theory that dominated educational thrusts for such a long time.

The cultural patterns of American society remained relatively homogeneous until the later part of the nineteenth century when a new group of immigrants, in addition to the Native Americans, Mexicans and Blacks appeared on the American scene. In both instances, the numbers at this time were not overwhelming. The non Blacks were either assimilated into the mainstream or given a place of "refuge" to live out their lives without undo interference from messengers of progress. The Blacks were "learning their places" and being relegated to them by the rise of segregated institutions. Economic development remained the major American interest and both the gradual transformation of an agrarian South and the rapid industrialization of the North created a demand for cheap labor.

Some of the "old" immigrants left the general labor force by becoming members of either the upper middle or upper class. Between this group and the less fortunate trouble erupted. These eruptions were based on "episodic economic decline, cruel conflicts between management and labor, and gross exploitation."[5] It was into this state of affairs that the new immigrants from eastern and southern Europe arrived. They were welcomed as new sources of cheap labor by the industrialists and subjected to hostile opposition by organized labor. In addition, they were different.

4

Differing from the earlier Anglo Saxons far more than the latter nationalities had differed among themselves, the new immigrants tended to settle in self contained communities that perpetuated the language, customs, practices and standards of their home lands . . . . A far higher rate of illiteracy was evidenced among these later immigrants . . . causing political and educational problems of the first magnitude in the cities where they settled.[6]

The new immigrant was labeled inferior and placed in somewhat the same category as the blacks. "The immigrants who arrived after 1880 struck the American imagination as a dark, swarthy, inferior race; they were drawn into the orbit of the associations linked to "black.""[7] Many of the racist beliefs about Blacks were expressed about the new immigrants. Though less obvious, violations of the civil rights of this group were widespread. The passage of the Thirteenth, Fourteenth, and Fifteenth Amendments to the Constitution provided protection for the rights of the new immigrants as well as the Blacks. The Civil Rights Act of 1875 made similar provisions.

Because Blacks were more numerous, more aware of the hostility of whites, and more distinctively colored, they were the most overtly harrassed and oppressed. Efforts for redress sought through judicial or legislative action were easily circumvented and often reversed. The Civil Rights Act of 1875 was recinded in principle and practice as soon as the federal troops left the South and were replaced with Jim Crow laws that stood until the latter part of the twentieth century. The doctrine of "separate but equal," based on the decision in Plessy v Ferguson (1896), sanctioned the existence of segregation that maintained its strongest bastion in the area of education. A dual system of education based on race was entrenched in the American educational system.

The "separate but equal" educational policy was most obvious in Black/white terms. However, its effect was subtly exerted on other non-western European groups. For example, in the controversy over universal education, little account was taken of the long tradition of highly developed educational systems in the native lands of some of the immigrants. From an extremist point of view, a system of universal education would not only lead to "mixing" but would breed immorality and related pathologies ascribed to inferior peoples. From a more liberal point of view, it was argued that universal education should not be handled through public schools. Reactions to both points of view led to the development of a number of exclusionary institutions and devices; for example, private schools and quota systems.

When public schools were finally established, the overt and covert belief in the inferiority inherent in differences developed, consciously or unconsciously, into institutional racism. Two separate school systems were maintained; one for whites and one for Blacks. Schools in other predominantly ethnic areas were slightly comparable to those for whites. The public sector was concerned with education as the vehicle for transmitting the cultural heritage, which by now had been clearly defined in terms of the Anglo Saxon middle class. Therefore, education became the major delivery system for "instant Americanization."

> What developed was a mass system of public indoctrination. That system had two functions: first, to create a lower laboring class . . . which adhered sufficiently to the values and myths of the American ruling class that it was not likely to question its place in society . . . . second, selection, the selection of those few, as needed who possessed adequate loyalty and sufficient conformity in attitudes, values, behavior, and appearance, to be adapted into the expanding middle class.[8]

The system espoused cultural indoctrination leading to cultural assimilation.

In short, the ethnic/cultural question was a private matter for the immigrants who were unwilling to assimilate and the Blacks who were unable to assimilate. Aware of existing inequities in the educational system but powerless to change them, these groups sought to improve the quality of the education they were receiving by establishing separate schools, attending parochial schools, and suggesting curriculum modification. Immigrant groups established and maintained by endowment private schools. Black education received institutional support from the philanthropy of persons such as Andrew Carnegie, Collis P. Huntington, Julia Rosenwald, John D. Rockefeller, and Caroline and Olivia Stokes, who were prominent supporters of industrial and agricultural education.[9] Elementary education for Blacks in rural areas was supported largely by the Jeanes Fund. Denominational groups established schools, with the Catholic school system being the strongest. Jewish groups provided religious and cultural studies during nonschool hours.

Schools established to meet the needs of Blacks and other culturally different groups were forced to exist under the aegis of the dual educational system. To achieve educational respectability or to receive accreditation, the curriculum of the schools had to conform to the cultural ethos of the dominant group. The culture of other groups—language, history, religion, etc.—was treated as electives. In extreme instances "it was unlawful in many states (until declared illegal by the Supreme Court in the Oregon Case) to teach a foreign language."[10] Whether education was obtained in public, private, or parochial schools, the ultimate goal was Americanization, which Novak defines as "a system of inhibitious and emotional responses that engender a cast of mind, a set of cues, an historical memory, a set of approved stories to live out."[11] In short, the educational system operationalized the melting pot theory.[12]

By the beginning of the twentieth century, the national effort was directed not only to building America but to creating Americans. Israel Zangwill's play, "The Melting Pot" (1909), provided the ideological label for the concept. The melting pot idea was consistent with the growing American nativism. "America is God's crucible . . . . the real American will be a fusion of all races."[13] Commager, as late as the middle of the century, pointed to the service provided by the public schools in bringing about the fusion.

> Each decade after 1840 saw from two to eight million immigrants pour into America. No other people had ever absorbed such large and varied racial stocks so rapidly or so successfully. It was the public school which proved itself the most efficacious of all agencies of Americanization—Americanization not only of the children but, through them, of the parents as well.[14]

Though the process of Americanization appeared to work, the myth of the melting pot was gradually being proved untenable. "The American melting pot did achieve reality in some instances—initially for the western European immigrant and later for his eastern European counterpart, but for the non-European, non white immigrant, the melting pot had little meaning."[15] To deal with the problem of the unmeltable immigrant, a series of immigration acts were passed. These acts set immigration quotas, restricted immigration on the basis of ethnic origin; and, in the case of Asiatics, excluded them from citizenship. These acts reflected the pervasive mood of nationalism that swept the country. They were removed from the statute books by the passage of the Reform Immigration Act during the Johnson Administration.

The problem of ethnic and cultural diversity no longer could remain either a private matter or a matter of fusion, Americanization. The American population was a unique combination of diverse cultural strains. A part of and apart from the idealized American, the immigrant and migrant elements of the population settled into ethnic and cultural enclaves. The meeting of the various cultural elements, however, produced conflict instead of cohesion. As a result, cultural unity, not cultural diversity, emerged as the prevailing idealized value. A "We"-"They" syndrome developed.[16]

Voices in America like those of John Dewey, Julius Drachsler and Horace Kallen were attempting to create among Americans an awareness of the richness of cultural diversity.[17] Possibly, an earlier voice was that of Booker T. Washington, who in the highly controversial Atlanta

Exposition Address, used a figure of speech that, divested of the external constraints imposed by Black/white relationships of the time, might well have foreshadowed cultural pluralism. Washington suggested that "we can be as separate as fingers, yet one as the hand in all things essential to mutual progress."[18] In a more universal context, the fingers could represent the distinctive ethnic cultural concerns of each group and the hand all things that operate in the general society for its enhancement and the improvement of the human condition.

Though it may be argued that interest in cultural diversity was aborted by the national concerns of the first half of the twentieth century, the fact remains that the events of the period led to greater cultural unity and greater disaffection with the mythical American dream. A World War and a great depression dramatized a cyclic movement within the country. After great bursts of patriotic endeavor in support of the shiboleth to make the world safe for democracy, the *status quo*—racism, poverty, and discrimination—was resumed. Blacks and other non-Caucasians were subjected to discriminatory practices under the courtupheld "separate but equal" doctrine. "There was nothing particularly secretive about . . . discrimination; it was an accepted way of life."[19] This way of life was, indeed, incompatible with a country that had established itself as a world power and the capstone of democracy.

It was, therefore, no mere coincident that overt signs of disaffection and unrest began to surface from among minority groups. Reaction to the unrest was "the development of a different sense of nationality: a concept accommodating and dignifying subnationalities and contributing cultures."[20] Reflecting this new awareness, the American society gradually began to move in the direction of pluralism as "an idealogy on the value level giving as an alternative to the 'One Great American Culture' idea the 'Many Great American Subcultures' program of pluralism, without any indication of how we are going to provide equal access to the sources of power for all or how we are going to learn each other's ways of interacting and communicating."[21]

Conditions in America in the years before and after World War II brought into sharp focus both the issues of interaction and power inclusion. Education, reflecting the concerns of the larger society, took clues from industry and the behavioral and social scientists and developed a growing interest in intergroup education. Much of the substantive work in this area may be attributed to the endeavors of Leland Bradford and Kenneth Benne who were primarily responsible for the development of human relations training, and to Hilda Taba who was one of the strong advocates of intergroup education in the public schools. Though the initial target population was Blacks, the results of much of the related

8

research were applicable to other racial and ethnic groups.

Concomitant with the interest in intergroup education was an interest in the education of the disadvantaged. Again, much of the related literature dealt with the effects of deprivation and racism on Blacks. Early research in the area was oriented, almost exclusively, to the pathology of Blacks. Later research documented the fact that the disadvantaged were as racially and ethnically diverse as the American population itself. More than 15 percent of the total population was disadvantaged, when the term was redefined to include "all persons who suffer from social and economic discrimination at the hands of the majority of the society."[22] Constituting the disadvantaged were the majority of Blacks, Mexican Americans, Puerto Ricans, Appalachian whites, and reservation Indians, all from largely rural backgrounds. Though, historically, members of these groups have been disadvantaged, it was not until they migrated in large numbers to urban industrial centers that they posed a real problem. The two major facets of the problem were the inability to adapt to the cultural ethos of the new community and the inability to adapt to the demands of a new technology. Much research pointed to education as the most viable solution.

Research findings, notwithstanding, judicial and legislative actions were required before any substantive action toward a solution was initiated. Actions with particular relevance to education included the following:

(1947) Publication of *To Secure These Rights*, the report of a Committee on Civil Rights appointed by President Truman. The report documented flagrant discriminatory practices in all areas of the society based on race, religion, and color.

(1954) Brown *v* Board of Education, a landmark decision by the U. S. Supreme Court. The Court, reversing Plessy *v* Ferguson ruled that separate educational facilities are inherently unequal.

(1957) Establishment of Federal Civil Rights Commission. The Commission, first empowered to deal with violations of voting rights, has had its powers extended to include violations of all civil rights.

(1964) Passage of Civil Rights Act. This Act spelled out the rights of individuals with regard to voting, employment, public accommodations, and education.

(1965) Passage of The Elementary and Secondary Education Act. The Act provided federal funding for the improvement of education and educational facilities for the disadvantaged.

9

(1966) Publication of the Coleman Report, *Equality of Educational Opportunity*. The report documented the lack of equal educational opportunities for minorities.

(1968) Publication of the report of the President's Commission on Civil Disorders. The report found white racism to be the major factor creating the frustrations of the powerless.

(1968-74) Study of Mexican American Education in the Southwest. The six year study tends to affirm Carter's description of Mexican American education as a history of educational neglect.

(1968) Bilingual Education Act (ESEA Title VII). The act provided for the training of teachers to work in bilingual programs.

(1970) U. S. participation in First International Education Year. Participating countries were urged to look at education in its broadest sense to promote equality of access to and treatment in education.

(1972) Publication of *On Equality of Educational Opportunity* by Masteller and Moynihan. The findings reported did not negate the conclusions drawn from the Coleman Report.

(1974) Lau *v* Nichols. The Supreme Court decision in this case established the right of a student to an education when his language is not English. The Bilingual Education Act was added as an amendment to the Elementary and Secondary Education Act of 1965.

In addition, legislative and judicial actions are either pending or being initiated relevant to the special concerns of women, the aged, young people, and Native Americans.

It would appear that the Civil Rights movement served as a catalyst for other racial, ethnic, and cultural groups. The movement engendered a new pride in ethnic and cultural heritages, created an awareness of the disparity of power and control, and called attention to the "culture of the powerless." In short, American culture could no longer be adequately defined as dual, either on the basis of social class or race, or on an ethnic or cultural basis. The dual concept overtly admitted the existence of a "superior" culture. From a more liberal stance, it subtly implies the existence of a "superior" culture, by juxtaposing other cultures with it on a continuum in rank order.

In terms of the educational system, the dual approach was proved to be no longer feasible. It was legally abolished by the decision in Brown *v* the Board (1954). Though many states resisted the change, the controversy still rages over related issues; the dual educational system has been proved incompatible with the contemporary cultural ethos. In its stead, pluralism has been embraced and implemented by a proliferation of hastily conceived, and often ineffectively implemented ethnic studies programs that not only fostered ethnic group ethnocentrism but led to power struggles between ethnic groups.

Few of the programs evolved beyond what Sizemore classifies as stage two, nationalism in the Power Inclusion Model.[23] The programs, operating adjunct to the educational program of the sponsoring institution, represented what Larry Cuban called "educational enclaves . . . without substantive changes."[24] The period of the seventies showed a decline in the number of ethnic studies programs, which appears to support Patterson's pluralistic fallacy: "emphasis on group diversity and group tolerance . . . fails to recognize a basic paradox in human interaction: the greater the diversity and cohesiveness of groups in a society, the smaller the diversity and personal autonomy of individuals in that society."[25]

Events of the past two decades have called for a reexamination of the concept of cultural pluralism. The larger society questions not only its efficacy but its reality as an achievable goal. Ethnic and cultural groups are becoming increasingly diverse within their own ranks. The dynamic underlying the proliferation of "cultures" within homogeneous ethnic and racial groups is the individual. As the individual achieves what Banks calls ethnic literacy,[26] he discovers that his identity is a composite of several "cultures," ethnicity being only one. It is possible that, at one and the same time, the individual interacts with the Black culture, the culture of poverty, the youth culture, and the urban culture.

Americans are beginning to realize that, like the country itself, they are multicultural, not only by racial and cultural mix but by identification with common needs, interests, and concerns. It is to this sense of identification that education must be developed. It must function within a changing social scene that is aware of and sensitive to cultural diversity and, at the same time, it must realize that all cultures interact with and may have implicit commonalities with all others. Education "must recognize the importance of educating individuals to behavior that reflects commonalities."[27] This type behavior can develop only when cultural differences are understood as different vantage points from which experiences are viewed, neither view being absolute or mutually exclusive.

To this end, multicultural education is an imperative for the American educational system. Multicultural populations, though most dense in urban areas, exist throughout the country. The schools, therefore, must concern themselves with the preparation of individuals to live in a society of varied races, cultures, and life styles, each different but interdependent. In spite of this fact, educational systems continue to vacillate between ethnic/cultural studies and cultural pluralism. Each approach has its merits, but each sanctions a degree of separateness that is contrary to the multicultural realities of society.

Philosophically, multicultural education should have as its focus the individual in a culturally pluralistic society. Ethnicity and culture, though integral parts of the individual's identity, must be viewed more broadly than as mere labels of group membership. Individuals are developing human beings, and the dynamics of human development involves interactions that are transcultural and transethnic. Multicultural education must address itself to the student who as an individual happens to be a member of a cultural or ethnic group. On the wider continuum of American society, the basic interaction is between individuals who perceive common needs and goals, sharing them in the process of self-actualization.

Pedagogically, multicultural education should include both the ethnic and pluralistic concepts in an educational environment, physical and social, that encourages an examination of cultural similarities and compatibilities. It must include both intercultural and intracultural emphases. According to Levine, if the individual can perceive himself as a part of a society that welcomes human diversity in appearance, belief, background, and custom he will, out of self-interest, act to reduce barriers that denigrate the dignity and integrity of others.[28] Some practices currently in vogue in education fail to take into account the inter-relationship between the individual's perception of the society in which he lives and the realities of that society. Multicultural education must be directed toward a resolution of the conflict.

Some definite steps have been taken in this direction. The American Association of Colleges for Teacher Education (AACTE) statement "No One Model American" suggested the philosophical and operational bases for culturally pluralistic education. It emphasized the "development of individual commitment to a social system where individual worth and dignity are fundamental tenets" within the context of "an educational program that makes cultural equality real and meaningful." Further, AACTE was supportive in promoting the inclusion of the Bilingual Education Act as an amendment to the Elementary and Secondary Education Act. Other professional organizations have embraced the concept of multicultural education. The National Council for the Social Studies, though its initial concern was ethnic studies, is in the vanguard of the movement toward multicultural education. Supportive efforts of other professional groups include, for example, the attack launched by the National Council of Teachers of English against racism in textbooks. The position statement of the Conference on College Composition and Communication, "Students' Right to Their Own Lan-

12

guage," provides another example. The 1974 meeting of Association for Supervision and Curriculum Development (ASCD) with the theme "Curriculum Action for a Crisis Society," had as one of its major problem thrusts multicultural education.

These efforts lend support to a conceptualization of multicultural education as the process through which cultural pluralism can be operationalized in the schools.

DIAGRAM A. *Cultural Pluralism Operationalized Through Multicultural Education*

The diagram attempts to provide a schematic representation of the conceptualization. The philosophy of cultural pluralism forms the hub of the wheel. The spokes radiating from the hub represent four general cultural factors that are substantively interrelated. Consideration of these factors constitutes an integral part of educational planning.

13

Instructional goals and strategies, multiethnic and sociocultural instructional materials, and humanistic learning environment, depicted on the outer rim, are, in fact, a matrix of elements designed to implement culturally pluralistic goals within an educational framework. The elements on the outer rim are cyclic, representing continuous interaction with the factors represented on the spokes. Therefore, the design indicates schematically that multicultural education is the perpetual action arm that provides an operational base for cultural pluralism.

The American culture is multifaceted. Each facet is essential to its totality and to heighten its richness and beauty. If the manifest function of American education is to transmit the cultural heritage, it must recognize the multifaceted nature of that heritage. Therefore, it seems safe to assume that the schools will become more responsive to cultural pluralism and committed to multicultural education as the vehicle for achieving goals consistent with the needs of the clientele they serve.

[1] Arnold Rose and Caroline Rose, *America Divided* (New York: Alfred Knopf, 1949), p. 50.

[2] R. Freeman Butts and Lawrence A. Cremin, *History of Education in American Culture* (New York: Holt, Rinehart, Winston, 1953), p. 117.

[3] See Eli Ginsberg and A. S. Eichner, *The Troublesome Presence* (Glencoe: Free Press, 1966).

[4] Michael Cole and Sylvia Scribner, *Culture and Thought* (New York: John Wiley, 1974), p. 17—parenthesis added.

[5] Michael Novak, *The Rise of The Unmeltable Ethnics* (New York: Macmillan, 1973), p. 95.

[6] Butts and Cremin, p. 306.

[7] Novak, p. 95.

[8] Mildred Dickman, "Teaching Cultural Pluralism," in James Banks, ed. *Teaching Ethnic Studies* (Washington: National Council for Social Studies, 1973), p. 6.

[9] Michael Winston, "Through the Back Door; Academic and the Negro Scholar in Historical Perspective," *Daedalus*, Summer 1971, p. 681.

[10] William Hunter, ed. *Multicultural Education Through Competency Based Teacher Education* (Washington, D.C.: AACTE, 1974), p. 14.

[11] Novak, p. viii.

[12] See Barbara Sizemore, "Shattering the Melting Pot Myth," in *Teaching Ethnic Studies*, James Banks, ed.

[13] Israel Zangwill, *The Melting Pot* (New York: Macmillan, 1907), p. 37.

[14] Henry S. Commager, "Free Public Schools—A Key to National Unity," in Henry Ehlers, ed. *Crucial Issues in Education* (New York: Holt, Rinehart, Winston, 1969), p. 6.

[15] William Joyce, "Minority Groups in American Society: Imperatives for Educators," *Social Education*, p. 430.

[16] See Peter Rose, *They and We: Racial and Ethnic Relations in the United States* (New York: Random House, 1974).

[17] See John Dewey, "Nationalizing Education," *Proceedings of NEA*, 1916; Julius Drachsler, *Democracy and Assimilation* (New York: Macmillan, 1920); Horace Kallen, *Culture and Democracy in the United States* (New York: Macmillan, 1924).

[18] Booker T. Washington, "Atlanta Exposition Address," in William Adamas, Peter Conn and Barry Slepian (eds.), *Afro-American Literature* (New York: Houghton Mifflin, 1970), p. 12.

[19] Henry Abraham, "Rise: The American Dilemma," in *Crucial Issues in Education*, p. 49.

[20] Hunter, p. 15.

[21] Roger Abrahams, "Cultural Differences and the Melting Pot Idealogy," *Educational Leadership*, Nov. 1971, p. 118.

[22] John Beck and Richard Saxe, *Teaching the Culturally Disadvantaged Pupil* (Springfield, Illinois: Charles Thomas Publishers, 1965), p. x.

[23] Sizemore, p. 82.

[24] Larry Cuban, "Ethnic Content and White Instruction," in *Teaching Ethnic Studies*, p. 113.

[25] Patterson, "Ethnicity and the Plural Fallacy," in *Change*, March, 1975, pp. 10-11.

[26] See James Banks (ed.), *Teaching Ethnic Studies* (Washington: National Council for the Social Studies, 1973).

[27] Paul G. Orr, "Internationalism and Interculturalism as Concepts," in Paul Olson, Larry Freeman and James Bowman (eds.), *Education for 1984 and After* (Chicago: Study Commission On Undergraduate Education and the Education of Teachers, 1971), np.

[28] Levine, "Imposed Social Position: Assessment and Curricular Implications," *Bulletin National Association of Secondary School Principals*, 1966, pp. 44-54.

Multicultural Education:
Definitions, Models & Issues

In this chapter, the writer will present various definitions of multicultural education and cultural pluralism. This will be followed by a description of several educational models that have been developed for the implementation of a cultural pluralistic philosophy via the multicultural process. The last section of this chapter explores some significant issues emerging from the process of multiculturalizing the educational system and the effect(s) the resolution of these issues may have on the future of multicultural education.

Multicultural Education Defined

The efforts of past and present day theorists have produced numerous programs designed to promote cultural diversity in education. As a spin-off, many conceptualizations of multicultural education have emerged. The literature is replete with definitions that reflect the coexistence of cultural diversity. Among the more definitive delineations are the following:

> Multicultural education is education which values cultural pluralism. Multicultural education rejects the view that schools should seek to melt away cultural differences or the view that schools merely tolerate cultural pluralism. Instead, multicultural education affirms that schools should be oriented toward the cultural enrichment of all children and youth through programs rooted to the preservation and extension of cultural alternatives. Multicultural education recognizes cultural diversity as a fact of life in American society, and it affirms that this cultural diversity is a valuable resource that should be preserved and extended. It affirms that major education institutions should strive to preserve cultural pluralism . . . .
> Education for cultural pluralism includes four major thrusts: (1) the teaching of values which support cultural diversity and individual uniqueness; (2) the encouragement of the qualitative expansion of existing ethnic cultures and their incorporation into the mainstream of American socioeconomic and political life; (3) the support of explorations in alternative and emerging life styles; and (4) the encouragement of multiculturalism, multilingualism, and multidialectism.[1]

The following statements on cultural pluralism express a human right to be culturally different without losing respect:

... Instead of the traditional view of equality of educational opportunity which stresses equal access to a single, universal school program, they advocate a pluralistic concept of equality which stresses respect for the diversity in cultural patterns and learning styles which is so widespread in America. These scholars raise serious questions about the ethical as well as the educational implications of policies that seem to devalue people who differ from the dominant groups . . . . Cultural pluralism involves the mutual exchange of cultural content and respect for different views of reality and conceptions of man. Pluralism assumes that ethnic groups have the right to preserve their cultural heritages and also to contribute to American civic life.[2]

... a state of equal co-existence in a mutually supportive relationship within the boundaries or framework of one nation of people of diverse cultures with significantly different patterns of belief, behavior, color, and in many cases, with different languages. To achieve cultural pluralism, there must be unity with diversity. Each person must be aware of and secure in his own identity, and be willing to extend to others the same respect and rights that he expects to enjoy himself.[3]

Havighurst analyzes the concept of cultural pluralism to include the following meanings:

1. Mutual appreciation and understanding of the various cultures in the society.

2. Cooperation of the various groups in the civic and economic institutions of the society.

3. Peaceful coexistence of diverse life styles, folkways, manners, language patterns, and religious beliefs, and family structures.

4. Autonomy for each subcultural group to work out its own social futures, as long as it does not interfere with the same right for the other groups.[4]

The historical reality of diverse people contributing to the greatness of this country is patently explicit in Williams' definition:

By cultural pluralism, I mean the realities of American history—the history that chronicles the struggles, tragedies, experiences, and contributions of all the peoples of the United States, the realities that indisputably illustrate that the blood shed in defending this country was and is culturally plural, that the tragedies of war and economic depressions were and are culturally plural, that initiative and responsibleness are experiences of *all* peoples of the United States, and that contributions to science and technology, economics, politics, literature, and the arts were and continue to be culturally plural.[5]

17

The definitions cited have binding commonalities: (1) a recognition and respect for diversity among people, (2) the value of human dignity and self-esteem, and (3) the preservation of cultural identity. Strongly implied in a definition of multicultural education or cultural pluralism, is the eradication of *racism*, along with its human destructive manifestations. Other terms, used synonymously, include cultural pluralism, cultural differences, cultural diversity, multiracial, and multiethnic. For the purpose of clarity, in this chapter the term multicultural or cultural pluralism will be used.

Educational Models and Implementation

Although paradigms for achieving a multicultural society, *via* the educational system, have been proposed by many leading educators, their primary focus often differs. The emphasis may be directed toward community involvement, pluralizing the curriculum, teacher training, or power acquisition. An in depth look at multicultural education necessitates an examination of some of the previously developed models— their format, function, rationale and possible effects. The models examined are not exhaustive. Other equally valid models exist, both in theory and in operation. The models selected, however, represent a unique prismatic view of the range of alternatives from which one may select implementation schemes for multicultural education.

Community

⊀ Educators are concerned about the manner in which their efforts are perceived by the community they serve. This concern is particularly relevant when the school administration and the school clientele represent diverse ethnic groups. Since the 1960's, many parents have sought viable avenues for involvement in educational activities that vitally affect the lives of their children. The CAPTS Model, developed in Chicago, was successfully utilized with an ethnically diverse population.[6] The model sought to provide a system whereby all segments of the school community could make their needs known and thus affect the decision making process.

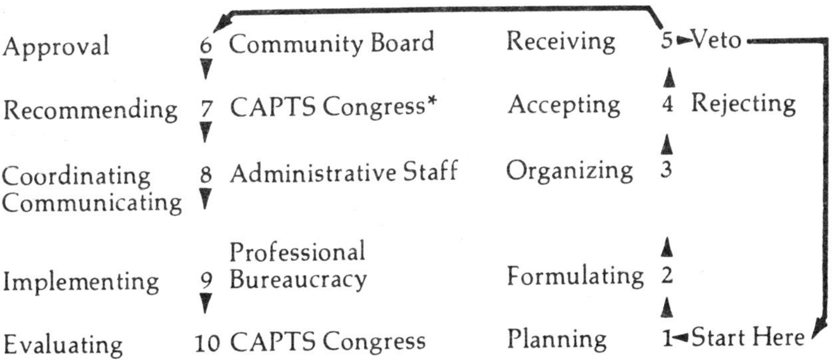

Approval	6	Community Board	Receiving	5 ►Veto
Recommending	7	CAPTS Congress*	Accepting	4 Rejecting
Coordinating Communicating	8	Administrative Staff	Organizing	3
Implementing	9	Professional Bureaucracy	Formulating	2
Evaluating	10	CAPTS Congress	Planning	1◄Start Here

FIGURE 1: *Community, Administration, Parents, Teachers, & Students

This ten-step model provided for the viability of each group while building the cohesion of the overall school community. Community leaders were provided an opportunity to be involved in educational planning. Teachers were able to establish lines of communication with community people, parents, and even the administration itself. Students were able to become a component of the model and react to programs and policies which directly affected them. This model becomes extremely important to urban and multicultural education because communities should not be forced to accept irrelevant and unsuccessful programs year after year.

Curriculum

Other educators have focused on the curriculum as the prime tool for achieving a multicultural society. Proponents of the curriculum focus include: James Banks who designed Curriculum Models for an Open Society; Carlos Cortés, who suggested that the curriculum move from traditional frames of references to exploratory concepts; and Francis Sussna who developed the Multicultural Institute.

The models for creating an open society devised by James Banks have some specific directions for curriculum developers.[7] Banks views society as composed of two factions, the oppressor and the oppressed. Education for an open society, he theorizes, cannot be accomplished by utilizing the same curriculum for both groups. Banks proposes that two separate curriculum strategies be followed: the Shared Power Model (for excluded groups) and the Enlightening Powerful Groups Model.

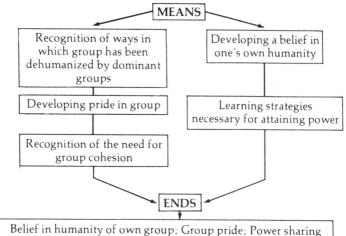

FIGURE 2: *Model I—Shared Power Model*

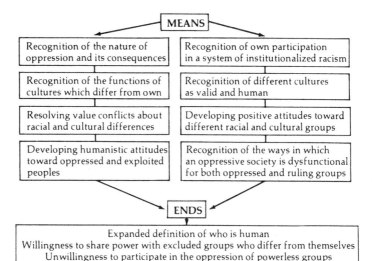

FIGURE 3: *Model II—Enlightening Powerful Groups Model*

Although the models appear in pure form, Banks cautions that strict adherence to one model is probably not possible; an eclectic use of both models might provide the best answer.

The Multicultural Institute[8] in San Francisco, was the result of tireless work by Francis Sussna, who became concerned about the manner in which culturally diverse people viewed each other. Developing cultural appreciation of one's own ethnic groups, while learning about other ethnic groups, is the curriculum challenge of the Multicultural Institute (MCI). Sussna's model provides for integrated classes and ethnic classes in which children master the basic skills and their respected cultures. The popularity and success of the Sussna approach has resulted in some public school districts adopting her multicultural curriculum. The Gatzert and Decatur Elementary Schools in Seattle and Canfield-Cresent Heights Community Schools in the Los Angeles area have implemented the MCI approach to the curriculum.

In designing a curriculum that effectively reflects the experience of ethnic groups, Cortés suggests that we reconceptualize the traditional frames of references and examine "exploratory concepts."[9] The Chicano experience is used as an illustration.

TRADITIONAL FRAMES OF REFERENCE	SUGGESTED EXPLORATORY CONCEPTS
1. U. S. history as an east-to-west phenomenon	1. Greater America concept
2. "Just like" explanations	2. Comparative ethnic experiences
3. Chicano homogeneity	3. Chicano diversity
4. "Awakening Mexican American"	4. History of activity
5. Heroes and success stories	5. The Chicano people

Cortés' model is important for all educators, not only those involved in an ethnic studies program *per se*, but also for those who teach by the "standard curriculum." Whether they realize it or not, all educators do reflect cultural experiences in the classroom. By omission of diverse cultural experiences, they communicate to their students that there is nothing of importance or value in the experiences of other cultures. The curriculum can contribute to the positive self-image of all students and further expand their understanding of the contributions of all people to the United States.

The Esperanza Model[10] is a three-stage model for developing a multicultural curriculum. The model was designed to aid school districts in devising a culturally pluralistic curriculum that would benefit all children.

The teachers exercise their professional skills and their cultural awareness in formulating plans for curriculum change from monocultural to culturally pluralistic. The community is solicited for aid and advice on educational projects. The developers of this model perceive it as offering a multi-faceted varied paradigm for reaching many different levels of the school community in effectively designing and implementing a curriculum reflective of cultural pluralism.

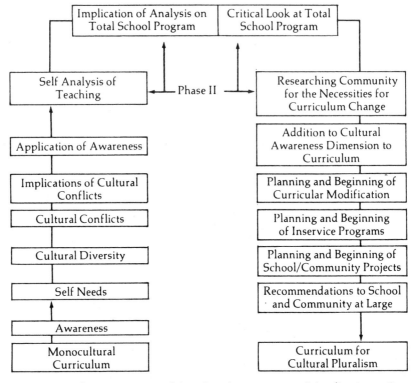

FIGURE 4: *The Esperanza Model: Cultural Awareness and Application to Curriculum*

Power

Some educators are concerned about the balance of power that operates in the larger society outside of the school. It is ultimately this society that children emerging from the school must deal with effectively. Barbara Sizemore has developed a power inclusion model[11] that would provide currently excluded groups the psychological, social, political, and financial cohesiveness necessary to gain parity in society. Dominant, powerful groups are referred to as *A* groups, in the Power Inclusion Model, and oppressed powerless groups are labeled as *B* groups. Extensive discussions of this model can be found in the literature.[12]

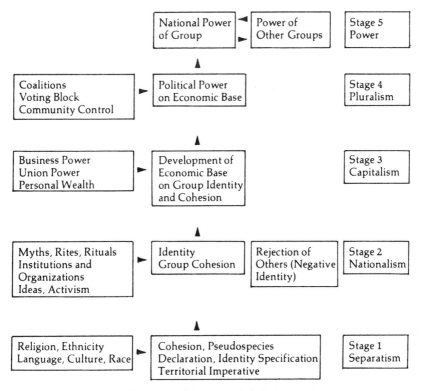

FIGURE 5: *Power-Inclusion Model for Excluded Groups*

Teacher Training

The Institute for Cultural Pluralism at San Diego State University has designed a teacher training model in multicultural education. The Community, Home, Cultural Awareness, and Language Training (CHCALT) Model[13] is divided into four basic components: (1)

philosophy of education for the culturally and linguistically different, (2) sociocultural awareness—home and community based, (3) oral language and assessment techniques, and (4) diagnostic and prescriptive strategies. During Phase I of the program, students are involved in a multidisciplinary (anthropological, sociological, psychological, aesthetic, linguistic, and historical) study of culture. Phase II places the students in the community of the target culture they have selected. This is followed by Phase III where the students evolve a thorough understanding of language from a cultural-community context, and the role of language as a vehicle for communication, cultural transmission, and sociocultural identification. In Phase IV, diagnostic and prescriptive strategies, students acquire the competencies to adopt and devise diagnostic tools and prescriptive strategies specified to meet the needs of the children they will teach (see Figure 6). The CHCALT Model is operationalized as a competency based individualized program. Students will be able to specialize in any one of the following cultures: Afro American, Asian American, Mexican American, and Native American.

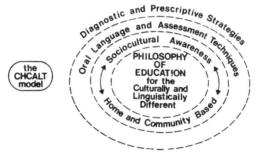

FIGURE 6: *Community, Home, Cultural Awareness, and Language Training*

The preceding models for achieving real and valid multicultural educational programs project some hypotheses for eradicating racist monocultural educational systems. The effectiveness of these models for achieving their chosen goals has not been measured. Their recency in both conceptualization and implementation, perhaps, prevents an objective evaluation of their effectiveness. Scholars of multicultural education must conceptualize, implement, and evaluate models of multicultural education. This must occur if basic changes are to occur in our educational system. No longer can we afford the "tack on process" of multiculturalizing educational systems by celebrating only Afro-American week, Latin-American day, and other symbolic futilities.

Basic Issues in Multicultural Education

Because of the lack of clarity concerning the meaning of the term "issues" itself, it is, perhaps, best to state at this point how the term is used within the context of this chapter. Here, the term issues refers to aspects of multicultural education concerning that on which a consensus has not been reached and about which debate in the scholarly and lay communities is still lively. This is hardly unusual. Whenever a new area of study makes its advent upon the educational scene, it is usually forced to undergo a process of legitimation. Programs in social studies and Black studies represent historical and current cases in point. In some instances, this process allows nonprogressive forces to prevent the introduction of critically needed innovations; but it also, sometimes, forces the proponents of a change for which an advocacy is being made to reexamine the theory and structure of their proposal and to write a scenario for its operation. A sound scenario provides both a preview of the major components of a program and an outline of the points on which major issues are likely to hang.

Any fruitful discussion of issues in multicultural education must concern itself with three dimensions: its origins, its current status, and its future. The first and third of these dimensions are discussed elsewhere in the chapter. Thus it is with the issues directed to its current status that we are at this point concerned. It is necessary, however, to note that because multicultural education seeks to move American education away from a dominant monocultural model toward utilization of models consistent with the cultural mix found in the population, it is in the broad spectrum of education, an issue itself. Yet, it is possible to identify six major areas within the multicultural universe around which critical issues have tended to center.

This much seems clear: the growth and stability of multicultural education, conceptually and operationally, depends primarily on the resolution of problems connected with (a) arriving at a suitable nomenclature, (b) establishing a viable organizational pattern and acquiring legitimation, (c) resolving the questions of who will teach multicultural education and how it will be taught, (d) developing suitable materials, (3) determining its relevance to the urban scene, and (f) financial support.

A basic issue that has prevented a clear understanding of multicultural education has been the myriad of terms by which it has been labeled. This excessive labeling reflects the amorphous character of multicultural education and the fact that it still has undefined parameters. This nebulous situation has led both its advocates and opponents to raise several basic questions: Is multicultural education a discipline of ethnic studies? Is it a philosophy? Is it cognitive or affective, or both? Is it compensatory education for minority racial groups? Perhaps, closely related to this labeling is the fear that multicultural education will become a euphemism for minority education. There appears to be a tendency among some educators to view multicultural education as a panacea for the "ills" of minority students. Under the guise of multicultural education, pathological approaches are spearheaded to cure the so-called psychological ills of minority children.

Establishing an agreed upon label is most important for communication purposes. Definitions cited earlier in the chapter clearly delineate this point. Yet, it seems proper to reinforce the point by indicating something of the dimensions involved since nomenclature has become a communications issue even among students of the subject itself. Further, the multiplicity of labels may well honestly confuse some educators and provide for others an excuse to maintain the *status quo*. Educators would do well to heed the admonition of Henry Steele Commanger who, writing in the special International Education edition of the *Kappan*, says that attempts of American schools to educate young people to a sense of membership in the human race have not produced the desired results because their "aim was not so much qualitative understanding as quantitative coverage."[14] If multicultural education is to avoid these pitfalls, parameters must be carefully defined and programs kept rigidly within the boundaries set.

Another issue in multicultural education is the form of organization it should follow. Should it be operationalized as a group of separate ethnic studies? This issue is inherent in the tendency of many colleges and universities to capitulate to the social and political pressures of minority ethnic groups to establish separate ethnic courses or programs. The most visible influences can be seen in the growth of Black and Chicano studies. A 1972 survey conducted by the New York *Times* indicated that at least 200 colleges and universities had established departments or special centers of Black studies. The Bilingual Education Act, recognizing the problems of Spanish-speaking people in the American Education System, gives rise to the establishment of ethnic studies programs from the elementary school to the university. In addition to these already well-established programs, Easy Klein, writing in *Change*, reports that "135 colleges and universities were offering 315 courses dealing with a wide range of national, religious and cultural groups .... added to curricula that already offered Black and Puerto Rican studies."[15] The proliferation of such offerings, in the light of the multicultural nature of the American society, is not to be condemned;

26

however, the very nature of their separateness falls short of the multicultural ideal and may portend the establishment of, what Larry Cuban calls, "educational enclaves without introducing substantive changes."[16] Hence, J. K. Obatala's finding that the number of separate Black Studies Programs existing in the 70's had declined in comparison with the number existing in the 60's[17] need not be an entirely negative phenomenon.

Such a finding could very well be an indicator of two positive spin-offs: the eradication of weak and ineffective programs and the absorption of some Black Studies programs in a broader more effective multicultural framework. Expectations for the immediate establishment of adequate and successful programs in any field were unrealistic. The case of multicultural studies was further complicated by the dubious circumstances of their origin. Originating largely as a pallative to minority student demands, they were designed basically to pacify rather than educate. Excellent programs do not originate over night. It is the nature of colleges and universities to establish priorities when handling programmatic thrusts. Usually this is done in response either to powerful pressure interest groups, or to a powerful white knight. Proponents of ethnic studies goals definitely could not follow the white knight model. Unfortunately, ethnic group ethnocentrism, along with narcissism, led to hostility between ethnic groups that prevented them from forming strong coalitions to exert pressure on the university, college, or school district. Subsequently, temporal reactive plans instead of permanent proactive plans were implemented. Therefore, in most cases, anemic separate ethnic studies programs were set up.

Crucial to this issue was and still is, in many instances, the student. Most of these programs were conceived with the coveted idea of serving a particular ethnic group to the outright exclusion of others. This approach ignored the idea that the purpose of ethnic studies was to enlighten all about a culture and its contributions. It was a fatal mistake for ethnic studies to attempt to serve one group at the exclusion of other groups. For, when the interest in the target group faded, so did the ethnic studies. In the author's judgment, the teaching of concepts from a separate entity instead of a pluralistic setting demeans the idea of cultural pluralism and the offering of separate ethnic courses as a program defeats the idea of an interrelated and integrated whole.

The strength of offering cultural pluralistic experiences lies in the sharing of cultural and ethnic experiences via generic concepts and topics. Another interesting issue results from the sectioning of bilingual education from multicultural education. A specific outgrowth of this issue is the multicultural-bilingual dichotomy. This dichotomy is being

27

promoted through financial support earmarked for bilingual or multicultural programs. Financially starved institutions responding to these monies foster this dichotomy. The tragedy of this dichotomy is that individuals who are committed to multicultural and bilingual education, begin to align themselves against each other along this false line of demarcation and expend their energies fighting each other for inadequate resources, when it would be wiser for the two to combine their efforts. The most excruciating problem within this issue stems from ignoring the primae facie relationship between culture and language. Language is not just a component of culture, its very essence comes from culture. The issue of separateness within multicultural education must be resolved if multicultural education is to develop fully and perform the service for which it was designed.

Another crucial issue is "who can or should teach in multicultural programs?" The issue revolves around the race and culture experiences. It is believed by some that unless you are a member of a minority group, you cannot be a valid instructor in multicultural education. As an illustration, some will say that only a Chicano can teach Chicano studies or only a woman can teach a course on women. It appears to the writer that this issue emanates from the "experience" philosophy. That is, unless you have experienced what it is to be a member of a particular cultural group, you cannot teach about that group. Such a point of view could lead to the conclusion that only an Englishman from England could teach English literature or English history. That should illustrate the absurdity of this idea so prevalent in ethnic studies today.

Further, this issue is reinforced by the willingness of employers (school districts, universities, colleges, federal agencies, etc.) to hire members of minority groups for positions related only to minorities or the disadvantaged, i.e., Upward Bound or minority studies. Subsequently, they support the preceding issue because it creates slots for minority ethnics which they do not want to hire anyway but must because of the Equal Employment Act. The implications of this issue are easily seen in education. Many non-minority teachers utilize this issue to escape having to multiculturalize their classroom activities. The crutch is that since they are not Black or they lack the "Black experiences," they cannot teach Black history. This becomes a paramount issue in teacher education when one realizes the number of teachers not teaching members of their own ethnic group and also not having the skills and competencies to provide a culturally pluralistic program. The typical teacher has a very narrow cultural base, that of the white middle class system permeated with ethnocentric snobbery. All teachers should have a culturally diverse repertoire of experiences, thus enabling them not only to relate positively to multicultural populations, but also to be able to provide multicultural experiences for their students. If teacher training is going to evolve in such a way that cultural pluralism becomes a major undergirding philosophy, then it is paramount that this issue be resolved.

At this time, perhaps the most obvious issue facing cultural pluralism is in the development of suitable educational materials (books, visual aids, teacher guides, etc.). The educational market has been flooded with materials reeking of *velvet racism*. That is, many "Dick and Jane" books have been revised to the extent that "Dick and Jane" now have two Black playmates, with nothing else having been changed in the book. The Coloring Game is abundant in educational materials. We find children's books which are actually reinforcing and constructing new stereotypes. The issue lies in the development of appropriate cultural pluralistic materials or the development of monocultural educational materials. It appears that the monocultural avenue is in vogue. An abundant amount of educational materials are being produced along a monocultural or monracial model, i.e., books on Chicanos, or slide tapes on Afro-Americans and poetry, of Native Americans or Irish Americans. Materials of this nature slow down the process of pluralizing the curriculum. If cultural pluralism is to make positive steps in curriculum development, then culturally pluralistic materials must be developed.

A sixth crucial issue is "who should be the recipient of multicultural education?" There are many who believe multicultural education is minority education. This is not true. Multicultural education is for *all* children. It is most important if we are to share this world peacefully that we share ourselves and our cultures. It is crucial for efforts in this direction to begin in the school, if not in the home. It is this sharing of cultures that can facilitate the eradication of racism. As long as children are fed stereotypes and false heroes, which tend to make one group feel superior to another, we will be cultivating racism and no doubt war. The absolute necessity of children learning about their own culture as they learn about other cultures should be bluntly logical. If not, then we are lost.

Undergirding the issues articulated here is the issue of financing multicultural education. Finance for programs of this type is usually provided by grants from the federal government or corporations and from the surplus "crisis" funds in the budgets of school districts. In the light of the tight money cycle when grants are fewer and the cross-cultural crises abates, at least on the surface, how will the programs sustain their existence? It is almost a truism in education history that a

29

course of study cannot become a viable and stable part of curricular structures until its support is based on regular or hard money allocations, and the agencies charged with the responsibility of legitimating programs have given it their approval.

The mention of these issues, by no means exhaustive, points to the urgency of legitimizing multicultural education as a viable part of the educational system. There are other issues and problems related to cultural pluralism, but it is beyond the scope of this chapter to discuss each of them. To indicate a few others, one must be mindful of the crucial role that testing has played in the miseducation of many children. Compensatory education is often times lumped into multicultural education and the preparation of trainers of teachers in a multicultural model must also be resolved. The urban community is but a microcosm of the multicultural world in which we live and education must produce a citizenry that can do more than just cope.

The Future of Multicultural Education

The writer views the future of multicultural education as speculative. The speculativeness of multicultural education graphically relates to the resolution of many of the issues discussed in the previous section. How these issues are resolved will determine the direction of multicultural education in the future. It is quite possible that a multicultural philosophy may become a very robust, intricate part of our education. For this to happen, several important decisions must be made concerning the institutionalized status, the politics of the multicultural/-bilingual dichotomy, research, teacher training, and a conceptualization of multicultural education. Besides the aforementioned decision variables, one must also consider multicultural education from an international perspective if it is to develop fully in the future.

In most institutions of education, universities, colleges, and school districts, multicultural educational programs are, at best, in limbo when it comes to determining their institutional status. They are either adjunct to major institutional programs or separate "add on's." They are supported by soft monies—federal, state, or local grants—that offer no assurance of year to year continuity. The very nature of this kind of funding prevents long-term planning and undermines the possibility of the program attaining full participation in the institution on par with programs funded by hard monies.

Linked to funding is the problem of program development. It is impossible for the staff to concentrate on long-term plans when each year

30

they have to compete for soft monies. If the future of multicultural education as a discipline evolving from a solid knowledge base is to be assured, multicultural education programs must be given full institutionalized status. This is basic to the livelihood of multicultural education. Unless this is accomplished, no proactive position can be taken in multicultural programs.

The politics emerging from the multicultural/bilingual dichotomy must be eliminated to prevent the extinction of both. It may well lead to a repeat of what happened to separate minority ethnic studies programs during the latter part of the 60's. It is both logically and philosophically sound for multicultural/bilingual programs to be encompassed under the same rubric. Logically, a study of culture involves an examination of linguistic patterns, including languages and dialects. Future developments in program designs for multicultural education should assure the inclusion of the language and dialect components along with other cultural components.

In the future, research must receive more emphasis. There is a need for the development of valid research models for multicultural education. Presently there is a paucity of research dealing with cultural pluralistic content, populations, teaching strategies, etc. It is common knowledge that the development of a discipline depends very heavily on research. In multicultural education, scholars must evolve modes of inquiry which will be proper for the problems related to multicultural education. The philosophy for research must move away from a preoccupation with pathological ideas about minority ethnic groups. Studies must be conducted from a cultural pluralistic vantage point in order to develop realistic knowledge results. In the past, most of the research in the antecedent area (culturally deprived, culturally disadvantaged), has been conducted in such a manner as to indicate "ills of the target population." Furthermore, this kind of research has usually been conducted from a monocultural perspective. Present research is usually characterized by a lack of pluralism. It will also be necessary to support research on a national scale to assure a broad base support system. Support of this type might well be achieved by the creation of a national research commission for multicultural education. The major purpose of the commission for multicultural education would be to generate research that would contribute to the development of multicultural programs. Another purpose of this commission would be to coordinate research on an international basis. A number of studies have been conducted in other countries utilizing methods applicable to culturally pluralistic programs. Linkage on an international level could be very beneficial to the evolvement of multicultural education within the United States.

The AACTE,[18] along with other teacher training endorsement agencies, is recommending and suggesting that teacher training programs include multicultural experiences. It is of paramount importance that teacher training programs are reconceptualized to include as a basic component an underlying philosophy of cultural pluralism. Although many teacher training programs are being reconceptualized under the competency based or performance based model, there is still a failure for them to include multicultural education as an integral component. Just espousing an acceptance of multicultural education is not sufficient. Competency based or performance based education must demonstrate its acceptance of a multicultural philosophy through the inclusion of this philosophy within all of its components. Unless this happens, teachers trained by these new conceptualized programs will not be any better trained to work in a culturally diverse urban society than those who were trained along traditional lines.

[1] "No One Model American," in *Journal of Teacher Education*, No. 4, Winter, 1973.

[2] Edgar G. Epps, "The Schools and Cultural Pluralism," in Edgar Epps, ed. *Cultural Pluralism* (Berkeley: McCutchan Publishing Corporation, 1974), pp. 176-177.

[3] Madelon D. Stent, William R. Hazard, and Harry N. Rivlin, "Cultural Pluralism and Schooling: Some Preliminary Observations," in Madelon D. Stent et al eds. *Cultural Pluralism in Education* (New York: Appleton-Century-Crafts, 1973), p. 14.

[4] Robert J. Havighurst, "The American Indian: From Assimilation to Cultural Pluralism," in *Educational Leadership*, April, 1974.

[5] Charles T. Williams, "Involving the Community in Implementing Cultural Pluralism," in *Educational Leadership*, December, 1974, p. 170.

[6] Barbara Sizemore, "Is There a Case for Separate Schools?" in *Kappan*, January, 1972, pp. 281-284.

[7] James Banks, "Curricular Models for an Open Society," in Delmo Della-Dora and James E. House eds., *Education for an Open Society*, Association for Supervision and Curriculum Development, Washington, D.C., 1974, pp. 43-63.

[8] Multicultural Institute Newsletter, Vol. 1, No. 2, 1974, San Francisco, California.

[9] Carlos E. Cortés, "Teaching the Chicano Experience," in James Banks, ed. *Teaching Ethnic Studies: Concepts and Strategies*, Washington, D.C.: National Council for the Social Studies, 1973), pp. 181-199.

[10] John Aragon, "An Impediment to Cultural Pluralism: Culturally Deficient Educators Attempting to Teach Culturally Different Children in Madelon D. Stent, William R. Hazard, and Harry N. Rivlin, eds. *Cultural Pluralism in Education: A Mandate for Change* (New York: Appleton-Century-Crofts, 1973), pp. 77-84.

[11] Barbara Sizemore, "Separatism: A Reality Approach to Inclusion?" in Robert Green, ed. *Racial Crisis in American Education* (Chicago: Fallet Education Corporation, 1969), pp. 249-279.

[12] James Banks, ed., *Teaching Ethnic Studies: Concepts and Strategies*, Washington, D.C.: National Council for the Social Studies, 1973), pp. 72-101.

[13] M. Reyes Mazon, "Community, Home, Cultural Awareness, and Language Training (CHCALT): A Design for Teacher Training in Multicultural Education," special report, Institute for Cultural Pluralism, San Diego State University, San Diego, California, 1974, 19 pages.

[14] Henry Steele Commanger, "Education and the International Community," in *Kappan*, January, 1970, pp. 231-232.

[15] Easy Klein, "The New Ethnic Studies," in *Change*, Summer, 1974, p. 13.

[16] Larry Cuban, "Ethnic Content and White Instruction," in *Kappan*, January, 1972, p. 273.

[17] J. K. Obatala, "Black Studies: Stop the Shouting and Go to Work," in *Smithsonian*, December, 1974, pp. 47-53.

[18] William A. Hunter, ed. *Multicultural Education Through Competency Based Teacher Education* (Washington, D.C.: AACTE, 1974).

33

BILINGUAL EDUCATION: THE STATE OF THE ART

I. Historical and Legal Background

In 1973, Texas and Illinois, following the earlier example of
Massachusetts, passed into law the Bilingual Education Acts. These
required the offering of bilingual instruction, grades 1-3, in all
public school districts with 20 or more limited English-speaking
children in any grade level. These Acts constitute a long-delayed
step aimed at overcoming years of educational neglect. From meager
beginnings, with limited knowledge, and with the legality provided
by law, bilingual education programs have expanded throughout the
United States. Today, both pedagogically and politically, bilingual
education has surfaced as one of the major issues of the decade.
Its rising visibility reflects the shifting political and philosophical movements within the United States. From the militant question-
ing attitudes of the 1960's wherein the traditional values of all
institutions were attacked and rejected, the pendulum swung to the
reactive attitudes of the 1970's during which the reality of institutional reform finally hit home. Today, the prevailing focus of
persons seeking to bring about desired changes must be on finding
ways of holding institutions accountable to the public they serve.
For educators then, ways must be found not only to keep our schools

---

This section was written by Dr. Victoria Bergen, Assistant Super-
intendent for Basic Curriculum Development, Houston Independent
School District, Houston, Texas

aware of changing students' needs, but also to ensure that there exists an institutional flexibility which allows schools to change in order to respond to these needs.

It is imperative that teachers, both practicing and aspiring, become aware of these issues as well as the historical background leading up to the present status of bilingual education. Without this understanding, the reality of daily classroom operation, especially the paperwork and guidelines required by mandated programs, becomes a confusing bureaucratic maze. The basic intent of these programs (better student achievement) often takes a back seat to what appears to be unrealisitc minority demands.

This paper will describe bilingual education in terms of the present state of the art, by scanning the historical and legal background leading up to the present, by describing the current implementation of bilingual programs, and finally by alerting the reader to the still relevant controversial issues which will hopefully be resolved in the years to come. Perhaps the very teachers who are reading this chapter will play leadership roles in helping to finalize the dream of equal educational opportunities for all children!

In 1965, Herschel T. Manuel documented amazing statistics related to the cumulative effect of poverty, low status, and lack of education on the Mexican-American. Average schooling was estimated at 4.8 years. Moreover, at every age bracket from five to nineteen, the lowest enrollment ratio was for Spanish-surname children. With each successive grade level, the ratio fell lower, reflecting the

35

phenomenon of "pushing" children out of school (Carter, 1970). The Governor's Commission on Public School Education in Texas (1968) reported the dropout rate for Mexican-Americans 78.2% for men, 79.7% for women. Traditional reasons for this lack of school success centered around a cultural deprivation theory which noted that (1) Enlgish cannot be mastered as long as the individual retains another language as the mother tongue; (2) using two languages as a medium of instruction causes academic retardation and physiological confusion; (3) the low educational achievement among Mexican-Americans is attributable to their retention of Spanish; and (4) retention of a foreign language impeded the Americanization of those who speak it. (Lara-Braud, 1970)

The U.S. Commission for Civil Rights Report entitled "The Excluded Student" (1972) verified the low achievement statistics reported above, but challenged the traditional assumptions related to causes for this low achievement. Indeed their documentation suggested that past practices in schools such as segregation, over-representation in special education classes, and discriminatory testing and placement practices, had served to sustain ethnic isolation, reinforce stereotypes, weaken students' sense of their own worth and, in fact, lowered student aspiration. The report suggested investigating alternative approaches (bilingual education among them) for meeting the needs of Spanish-speaking students. Even then, some research was reporting that children not only learned better initially in their mother tongue, but that the transition to a second language could best be accomplished when built upon a

36

reading and writing base in the native language. In other words, if the goal of the educational system was to teach a child to read and write in English, it was axiomatic that this could best be accomplished by teaching the child to read and write first in the language which the child spoke.

While such unorthodox views were being aired by educators throughout the world, proponents of bilingual education were still few and far between in the United States. Issues that were brought up before public arenas focused on the problem rather than on solutions. Indeed many children were not making it through the educational system! Indeed many children were either failing, dropping out, or being "pushed out" of the educational system! Most of these students were either ethnic or language minority students. While some isolated bilingual programs were being implemented as pilot programs around the country, the usual solution to the problem of low achievement centered on compensatory programs for language minority children: more Head Start, more remedial programs, more special education programs.

The Civil Rights Act of 1964 spoke directly to the educational practices of schools insofar as minority children were concerned. Specifically Title VI, Section 601, of the Civil Rights Act stipulated that no person was to be discriminated against on the basis of race, color, or national origin in any program receiving federal assistance. The intent of this provision was to insure that all individuals had equal access to federally sponsored programs. Since many school districts (particularly those with minority students) were recipients of federal funds, this provision obliged districts to submit documentation showing that the programs were nondiscriminatory.

Few people could foresee at the time that this Act would become a principal weapon for establishing bilingual programs. A national consciousness and understanding of the need for bilingual eudcation had not yet been established (Teitelbaum, 1977). Moreover, in 1964 relatively few school districts were actually receiving federal monies. Therefore, the threat of Title VI non-compliance was not relevant to those districts. Still, the foundation had been laid which would later provide the strength for subsequent implementation of bilingual programs.

In 1965, the Riverside Study (Mercer, 1972) supported similar findings throughout the country that Spanish-speaking minorities were being assigned to classes for the mentally retarded on the basis of their inability to speak English. The following year, the Coleman Report (1966) documented for the public the failure of our public school system to provide appropriate educational programs for all students. Both studies are important in that through their wide dissemination educators, politicians, lawyers, and advocacy groups throughout the nation became glaringly aware of the magnitude of the problem and its tragic consequence for minority groups. Public dialogue followed. Specific concerns relating to language minorities were given wide public hearings. Pressures were exerted to increase the base of funding for bilingual programs.

The passage of the Bilingual Education Act of 1968 provided a legal way to address the needs of language minority children through bilingual instruction. Specifically, Section 702 of the Act stated that:

> In recognition of the special educational needs of the large numbers of children of limited English-speaking ability in the United States, Congress hereby declares it to be policy of the United States to provide financial assistance to local educational agencies to develop and carry out new and imaginative elementary and secondary programs designed to meet these special educational needs. For the purposes of this title, "children of limited English-speaking ability" means those who come from environments where the dominant language is other than English.

Through the Bilingual Education Act, monies were provided for establishment of bilingual instructional programs, development of bilingual curriculum and materials and bilingual teacher training. Such monies provided the legal encouragement for school districts to conceptualize alternative language programs for limited English-speaking ability or bilingual students. The major thrust for expanding the implementation of bilingual programs was not underway!

In 1970, a suit was brought by Chinese public school students against the San Francisco Unified School District. This suit, Lau v. Nichols, questioned whether or not non-Engligh-speaking students receive an equal educational opportunity when they are instructed in a language which they do not understand. The plaintiff's presentation rested largely on Title VI guidelines and on the government's right to place reasonable conditions on the receipt of federal monies and on the Constitutional right to equal protection under the law. (It should be noted, that by 1970, given the impetus of the Bilingual Education Act, many more school

39

districts were receiving federal monies than had been in 1964 when the Civil Rights Act was passed). Lau V. Nichols went to the Supreme Court, which in 1974, basing its decision on Title VI of the Civil Rights Act, ruled that "There is no equality of treatment merely by providing students with the same facilities, textbooks, teachers, curriculum, for students who do not understand English are effectively foreclosed from meaningful education." Following the ruling, a task force was set up to delineate procedures insuring the proper use of assessment techniques and educational policies for non English-speaking students. The Task Force Findings (1975), which later became known as the Lau Remedies, specified that a student's linguistic functioning must be assessed in terms of one of the following five categories:

1. Monolingual speaker of the language other than English (speaks the language other than English exclusively).

2. Predominate speaker of the language other than English (speaks mostly the language other than English, but speaks some English).

3. Bilingual speaker (speaker both the language other than English and English with equal ease).

4. Predominate speaker of English (speaks mostly English, but some of a language other than English).

5. Monolingual speaker of English (speaks English exclusively).

Additionally, after identifying and categorizing students, school districts were required to develop an educational plan compatible with the student's linguistic needs. (Suggested educational plans will be discussed in the following section). The impact of this ruling was felt in school districts throughout the country as bilingual programs expanded rapidly. The focus on bilingual instruction in turn mandated increased in bilingual teacher training programs, bilingual textbooks, bilingual testing instruments, and bilingual support services.

The implementation of bilingual programs in many different languages is now an established educational alternative throughout the country. Between 1968 and 1969, seventy-six bilingual projects in fourteen languages were implemented throughout the United States to serve a total of 33,732 students. By 1976, a total of 406 bilingual projects focusing on forty-seven different languages had been implemented to serve a total of 206,452 students (Blanco, 1977). It is certain that these numbers will greatly increase in the years to come. Although federal funding provided the original impetus to implement bilingual programs, efforts at the local and state levels must be duly recognized. Moreover, curriculum areas such as reading, mathematics, social studies, and foreign language have rallied around the cause of a multilingual and multicultural educational delivery system. From meager beginnings which were based on a misguided notion that compensatory or remedial programs were the only vehicles for addressing the needs of language minorities, educators throughout the country have focused their attention on forcing an institution to change and adapt itself to the varied needs of its students. In the final analysis, bilingual education is the same as regular education. It is the necessary step which must be taken to insure equal educational opportunities for all children.

41

II. Current Implementation

What is bilingual education? One commonly accepted definition

has been set forth by the U.S. Office of Education (197]):

> Bilingual education is the use of two languages,
> one of which is English, as mediums of instruction
> for the same pupil population in a well-organized
> program which encompasses all or part of the
> curriculum and includes the study of the history and
> culture associated with the mother tongue. A complete
> program develops and maintains the children's
> self-esteem and a legitimate pride in both cultures.

Most states that have passed bilingual legislation have delineated

bilingual program components similar to those of the Texas

Education Agency (1974) which stipulate that:

> Bilingual education is a full-time program of
> instruction developed to meet the individual needs
> of each child in order that the pupil can parti-
> cipate in the regular school program as rapidly as
> possible. It is characterized by the following
> instructional components:

> 1. The basic concepts initiating the child into the
>   school environment are taught in the language he
>   brings from home.

> 2. Language development is provided in the child's
>   dominant language.

> 3. Language development is provided in the English
>   language.

> 4. Subject matter and concepts are taught in the
>   child's dominant language.

> 5. Subject matter and concepts are taught in the
>   English language.

> 6. Specific attention is given to develop in the
>   child a positive identity with his cultural her-
>   itage, self-assurance, and confidence.

42

While most state plans included the specific delineation of all the above components, school districts had difficulty in the practical implementation of bilingual programs. Because of the various approaches which were actually in operation throughout the country, and as a response to requests for specific guidelines, the Task Force Findings Specifying Remedies Available for Eliminating Past Educational Practices Rules Unlawful under Lau V. Nichols (Lau Remedies) were issued in the summer of 1975 to provide guidelines for the delivery of appropriate instructional services to limited English-speaking ability children, based on their language categories. These guidelines suggested the following approaches:

I. Initiation of systematic procedures to identify the student's primary or home language

Categorization of the student in one of the following categories:

A. Monolingual speaker of the language other than English
B. Predominate speaker of the language other than English
C. Bilingual
D. Predominate speaker of English
E. Monolingual speaker of English

II. Diagnostic/Prescriptive Approach

The district must describe the diagnostic/prescriptive measures to be used in identifying the nature and extent of each student's educational needs. An educational program must then be designed for each student.

III. Educational Program Selection

In this critical phase of the Lau process, appropriate types of educational programs must be prescribed for students depending upon their degree of linguistic proficiency.

*Guidelines for appropriate program selection are as follows:

A. Monolingual speaker of the language other than English
   (Elementary)

   Transitional Bilingual Program
   Bilingual/Bicultural Program
   Multilingual/Multicultural Program

   Monolingual speaker of the language other than English
   (Secondary)

   Subject matter instruction in the native language
      and ESL
   High Intensive Language Training (HILT)
   Bilingual/Bicultural Program or Multilingual/
      Multicultural Program

B. Predominate speaker of the language other than English
   (Elementary)

   Transitional Bilingual Program
   Bilingual/Bicultural Program
   Multilingual/Multicultural Program

   (Secondary)

   If the students who have been in the school system
   for a year or more are underachieving, the district
   must submit a plan to remedy the situation. This
   plan must include any one or a combination of the
   following:

   English as a Second Language (ESL)
   Transitional Bilingaul Education Program
   Bilingual/Bicultural Program
   Multilingual/Multicultural Program

   These students may not be placed in situations
   where all instruction is in the native language,
   however. Since they are secondary students,
   time is critical. They must be moved into the
   English instructional component as quickly as
   possible.

C. Bilingual speaker

   Treatment is the same as with the category A and

and B speakers. It differs only in terms of under-
achievers and those students achieving at grade
level or over.

Underachieving: Treatment corresponds to the regular program requirements for any student who requires
special program support, regardless of his/her
language background.

On grade level or better: The district is not required to provide additional educational programs
for these students.

D. Predominant speaker of English

Treatment for these students is the same as C, above.

E. Monolingual speaker of English

Treatment for these students is the same as C, above.

IV. Required and Elective Courses

In the fourth step of this plan, the district must show
that limited English-speaking ability students are not
placed in a special track which would isolate them from
the rest of the school program. Limited English-
speaking ability children must be placed in programs
which are not racially identifiable. They must have
access to elective courses and co-curricular activities
which are available to other students.

V. Instructional Personnel Requirements

Instructional personnel teaching the students in question
must be linguistically and culturally familiar with
the background of the students.

The student/teacher ratio for these programs should be
at least equal to that of the district.

If the district does not have adequate staff to implement
appropriate programs, a plan must be submitted by the
district, delineating steps which are to be taken to
insure the hiring and/or training of such staff.

VI. Racial/Ethnic Isolation and/or Identifiability of Schools
Classes

It is not educationally necessary nor legally per-
missable to create racially/ethnically identifiable
schools in order to respond to student language

characteristics as described by Lau.

VII.   Notification to Parents of Students Whose Primary or Home Language is Other Than English

School districts must inform all minority and non-minority parents of all aspects of the programs designed for students of limited English-speaking ability, and that these programs constitute an integral part of the total school program.

VIII.   Evaluation

The Regional Office of the Office of Civil Rights requires that a school district submit a progress report sixty days after school starts which shows those steps which have been completed in identifying students and assigning them to appropriate programs. Another progress report is due at the close of 30 days after the last day of the school year in question.

Definition of Terms:

1.   English - as - a - Second Language (ESL)

This is a structured language acquisition program designed to teach English to students whose native language is not English. ESL is a required component of ALL bilingual programs. Specific methodology includes an emphasis on oral language development, pattern and substitution drills, and a synthesis of approaches used in both foreign language teaching and English teaching.

2.   High Intensive Language Training (HILT)

This is a total immersion program designed to teach students a new language. It utilizes ESL methodology on a more intense basis and for a longer period of time each day. The main objective of this program is to have the student functional in English as quickly as possible. This type of approach has been highly successful with motivated salesperson, business person, military personnel, etc., who must make a rapid transition into a new language.

3.   Transitional Programs

A transitional program is one in which the native language is used only until a student is able to participate in academic subjects in English. Most bilingual programs in the United States are transitional. State and federal legislation generally supports the implementation of compensatory or transitional approaches.

4. Maintenance Programs

Maintenance programs have as their main objective, fluency and literacy in both languages. Students are taught not only reading and writing, but also content areas in both languages. Most European bilingual programs are maintenance programs.

5. Bilingual/Bicultural Programs

A Bilingual/Bicultural program is one which utilizes the student's native language and cultural factors in instructing, maintaining and further developing all the necessary skills in the student's native language, while introducing, maintaining and developing all the necessary skills in English. A Bilingual/Bicultural Program may operate as a maintenance or transitional model, depending on whether or not the native language is phased out once the student can function in English.

6. Multilingual/Multicultural Program

This is a program operated under the same principles as a Bilingual/Bicultural Program, except that more than one language and culture, in addition to English language and culture is treated. The end result is a student who can function in more than two languages and cultures.

7. Underachievement

Underachievement is defined as performance in each subject at one or more standard deviations below district norms as determined by some objective measures for non-ethnic/racial minority students. Mental ability scores cannot be utilized for determining grade expectancy.

8. Instructional Personnel

Persons involved in teaching activities. Such personnel includes credentialized teachers, para-professionals, teacher aides, parents, community volunteers, youth tutors, etc.

The Lau Remedies have described for districts, specific steps which must be taken to insure equal educational opportunities for limited English-speaking ability students. Most bilingual programs

47

which are currently in operation in the United States, are
attempting to follow closely those steps which have been summarized
above. In spite of the political spotlight on target languages,
the primary emphasis of bilingual education does rest within
the cognitive and affective, rather than the linguistic domains.
In other words, the main purpose of bilingual education is not
to teach language, but rather to enable students to learn content
and skills in the language that they understand, while at the same
time learning English. It is not necessary for a student to sit
in a classroom for two or more years - learning little - while
he attempts to learn English on his own. He can continue to
make progress, along with his peers, in the content areas as he
learns English. If the reader will recall the historical background behind implementation of bilingual education, the primary
legal thrust was to enable a student to participate successfully
in the educational process. In practice, the implementation of
appropriate programs for limited English-speaking ability children
must focus on ways of developing and maintaining their skills
while, at the same time, insuring their introduction to, and
mastery of the English language.

III. Future Concerns

We have seen that the expansion of bilingual education has
not peaked. Indeed the state of the art should be considered in
its infancy. What will the future hold?

Clearly we can predict a tremendous expansion of bilingual
programs to include many languages. The impact of the Lau Remedies

which were only published in 1975, has still not been felt in all areas. The ever-increasing influx of foreigners throughout the country has added additional numbers to the already large numbers of potential limited English-speaking ability students. The 1976 totals of 406 different projects focusing on forty-seven different languages (Blanco, 1977) represented only federally funded projects. The Lau Remedies point out that programs must be provided by districts through local funds, regardless of the availability of federal funds. It can be predicted that the 1980 totals will possibly double the totals of 1976.

Additionally, our increasing dependency on foreign oil as well as international business and cultural contacts, have resulted in an awareness of this country's lack of language resources. Foreign language enrollment has declined to an all-time low in the past few years. The trend cannot continue if we are to maintain our leadership position, politically and economically, in the world.

Finally, the growing visibility of bilingual politics has created an arena through which language minorities, who traditionally were unheard, have been able to articulate their aspirations and concerns. Parents who, themselves, gave up their language and culture in order to become part of mainstream culture, are asking that their children be given the opportunity to embrace both cultures. Parents in different communities are recognizing not only the cultural benefits, but the future financial benefits, of bilingualism. They are demanding bilingual programs for their children whether they qualify for them or not. In other words, some parents are demanding enrichment bilingual programs as opposed to compensatory bilingual programs.

All of these forces taken together, indicate that the movement for bilingual education will continue to grow during the next decade at a pace beyond which our resources can extend. Rapid expansion will bring with it many problems which are barely visible at the present time. Let us examine some of the concerns which will emerge in the next few years.

Staffing

Clearly one of the critical shortages of the next few years will be in the personnel necessary to staff not only the mandated programs, but those which can be predicted will be implemented as enrichment programs. Universities will have to gear up their resources to meet the demand for trained bilingual teachers, counselors, supervisors, etc., in various target languages. It is possible that the foreign language requirement for college graduation may be reinstated in all areas, for not only bilingual teachers will be needed to teach in basic "bilingual" classrooms, but math specialists, science teachers, music and art instructors; in fact, all areas of education will feel the impact of bilingual programs and will require the availability of specialists in any number of fields who are also fluent in another language. Certainly, increasing employment opportunities for bilingual personnel, in business, education, and technical fields, will create pressure

50

not only on the universities to provide language training,
but in turn, will create pressure on public schools to begin
language training at secondary and possibly elementary levels.

Bilingual Education and Special Education

Mention has been made of past research regarding the over-
representation of Spanish-speaking children in mentally retarded
classes because of discriminatory testing which measured English
proficiency rather than intelligence. This issue has not been
settled, in fact, it promises to be one of the great issues of
the next several years. A case which had great impact on policies
effecting the assessment of language minority students was Diana v.
California State Board of Education. In this case the plaintiffs
for nine Mexican-American children, ages 8 to 13, claimed they
had been improperly placed in classes for the mentally retarded
on the basis of IQ scores derived from the Stanford-Binet and
Wechsler Intelligence Scale for Children. After being tested
bilingually, seven of the nine students no longer were within the
retarded range. An out-of-court settlement in 1970, required that
in the future all children be tested in English and their primary
home language. Additionally it required that each school district
in California submit to the state a summary of retesting and re-
evaluation of children whose home language was other than English,
and that norms for a new or revised IQ test be developed to reflect
the abilities of culturally and linguistically different children.
Subsequent litigation in other states resulted in legislation aimed

51

at providing equal access to education through appropriate testing and programs for non-English-speaking handicapped students. Public Law 94-142 has attempted to address this issue by providing every possible safeguard against inappropriate placement. However, the impact of this legislation has often resulted in expanded and often cumbersome administrative procedures which, while ostensibly aimed at appropriate placement for non-English-speaking handicapped students, has served to protect districts from lawsuits, should placement of students be questioned. In many districts, an unusual phenomenon has surfaced. Bilingual teachers are complaining about the increased placement of handicapped youngsters in bilingual classrooms. In an almost complete turnaround from the days in which discriminatory over-representation of Spanish-speaking youngsters in special education classes was the issue, there is emerging a concern that limited English speaking ability children who need special education placement are not being appropriately screened or placed. Reasons for this under-representation now focus on the lack of appropriate instrumentation, and more specifically, the lack of bilingual special education personnel. The problem is critical. Given the already-established lack of sufficient bilingual teachers, it can only be assumed that the lack of sufficient bilingual special education teachers is even more critical. The needs of bilingual handicapped students must be met.

Institutionalization of Bilingual Programs

The passage of the Bilingual Education Act of 1968 provided

funding for the implementation of bilingual programs throughout the country. Since that time, most bilingual programs have been established out of the financial base provided by specialized funding. Even where programs have been funded out of local or state funds, the program's administration has focused on separating it from the rest of the school and/or district's operation. In many districts, a specialized Bilingual Department exists to handle the needs of a specifically identified population. All concerns relating to this population are referred to the Bilingual Department, with little communication existing between the Bilingual Department and other departments who should also be assuming responsibility for these same students. It can be predicted that as programs expand and as more students are "phased out" of bilingual programs to regular English classrooms, it will become increasingly necessary to examine lines of communication and administrative structures in order to avoid any vestiges of a dual Bilingual/non-Bilingual system and in order to truly implement a unitary system which is sensitive to different students' needs.

As teachers have become involved in the process of moving students from one category to another, it has become obvious that many similar problems exist in the regular English classroom as in the bilingual classroom. Many of the techniques which are appropriate for English-as-a-second language, for example, are appropriate for English monolingual students who are having difficulty with English reading. As another example, a bilingual teacher may be able to communicate with the student in his/her own language, but may not be sufficiently knowledgeable about

mathematics instruction to recognize when the student is
having difficulty with a mathematics sequence rather than
with language. The additional help of a mathematics specialist
may be necessary. In cases such as this, and many others, it
is necessary that curriculum between the two programs be carefully coordinated, and that all school personnel communicate
about all the students for whom they are collectively responsible.

In the final analysis, a bilingual program must be considered,
not as a separate program or track, but as one component of the
total instructional program offered in the school. Research
services should coordinate information about all students in
the district, including those in the bilingual programs. Curriculum specialists should consider all students in the district
when they are developing curriculum, including those in the
bilingual programs. Local funds should be distributed equitably
to all students in the district in accordance with their needs.
Only by a total coordination of district-wide efforts to focus
on the needs of all children and to look at the total population as a whole, rather than in terms of isolated programs,
can the resources of a school district be effectively deployed
to meet legislated mandates and at the same time address student
needs. Separate programs. separate tracks, only serve to
isolate children, thereby making it more costly and difficult
to move them into the mainstream of the educational program.
Bilingual programs, because of the funding emphasis and also
because of the degree of separateness inherent in speaking

54

different languages, have begun their existence as generally isolated programs. It can be predicted that the future will see an institutionalization of these programs as they become part of the regular program offerings of a district.

Possibly no educational innovation has had as great an impact on our social and political lives as bilingual education. Certainly, none has been as controversial. The controversy still exists. While there are those who believe that bilingual eudcation is un-american, and designed to subvert american values, there are few who, after having observed it in action, still maintain that it is not the best possible approach for those children who do not understand English. Who could contend that it is better to let children sit in class for several years, ignorant of what is going on around them, while they learn English in a non-systematic, casual way? As with any new program, there is still much to learn. Mistakes have been made. Programs have not always been implemented as they might have been under more ideal circumstances. The lack of bilingual staff has posed a severe hardship on implementation. Still, a giant step has been taken towards recognizing the needs of limited-English-ability children. More than that, a giant step has been taken towards recognizing the fact that we do live in a cultural pluralistic society and that our strength lies not in our ability to mold everyone to the same pattern, but in our ability to draw from our unique differences for the common good.

References

Bilingual Education Act, 20 U.S.C. 880b. Enacted January 2, 1968, P.L. 90-247, Section 702.

Blanco, George. "The Education Perspective" in Bilingual Education: Current Perspectives, Center for Applied Linguistics, November 1977, p. 18.

Carter, Thomas P. Mexican Americans in School: A History of Educational Neglect (New York: College Entrance Examination Board, 1970) pp. 20-23.

Civil Rights Act of 1964, U.S. Congress, P.L. 88-352.

Coleman, J. and others. Equality of Educational Opportunity. Office of Education, Department of Health, Education and Welfare. Washington, D.C.: U.S. Government Printing Office, 1966.

Diana v. California State Board of Education. No. C-70 37 RFP, District Court of Northern California (February 1970).

Governor's Commission on Public School Education: The Challenge and the Change, Austin: State of Texas, 1968, p. 16.

Manuel, Herschel T. The Spanish-Speaking Children of the Southwest - Their Education and the Public Welfare (Austin: University of Texas Press, 1965) p. 55.

Lara-Braud, Jorge. "Bilingualism for Texas: Education for Fraternity," Austin: Hispanic-American Institute, 1970. (Mimeo) p. 2.

Lau v. Nichols, 414 U.S. 563, 1973.

Mercer, J.R. The origins and development of the pluralistic assessment project. Unpublished manuscript, 1972. (Available from J.R. Mercer), UCLA, Los Angeles.

Senate Bill 121, Sixty-third Legislature (Sub chapter L, Chapter 21), Texas Education Code, 1974.

Task Force Findings Specifying Remedies Available for Eliminating Past Educational Practices Ruled Unlawful Under Lau v. Nichols. Washington, D.C.: DHEW/Office of Civil Rights, 1975.

Teitelbaum, Herbert and Richard Hiller, "Bilingual Education: The Legal Mandate," Harvard Educational Review, V. 47, May, 1977, p. 140.

U.S. Commission on Civil Rights Report III, The Excluded
Student: Educational Practices Affecting Mexican Americans
in the Southwest, May, 1972.

U.S. Office of Education. Programs under Bilingual Education
Act: Manual for Project Applicants and Grantees, 1971.
Washington, D.C.: U.S. Government Printing Office.

Mini-Reviews of Selected Readings in Multicultural Education

Andersson, Theodore and Mildred Boyer. *Bilingual Schooling in the United States.* 2 vols. Austin, Texas: Southwest Educational Development Laboratory, 1970.

This monograph is designed basically as a guideline for those planning bilingual programs. The monograph is quite useful but sketchy in areas dealing with a history of bilingual education in the United States and other parts of the world. There are also presented sound alternative concepts of bilingual schooling, sample curriculum models, and an outline of the need for bilingual education.

Banks, James A. and Jean D. Grambs, eds. *Black Self-Concept,* New York: McGraw-Hill Book Co., 1972.

Banks and Grambs have put together a series of essays which approach the problem of education and Black self-concept from different perspectives. The underlying thesis of the book is a concern with creating a school environment which can facilitate the attainment of positive and healthy self-concepts by Black children. The several authors discuss the effects of racism, the Black revolt of the 1960's, the relationship between social science, education, and Black identity on Black self-concept. The different perspectives also clearly show that there is no consensus about what self-concept is. And the editors clearly admonish a standardized definition of self-concept before conclusive statements about Black self-esteem can be made.

Banks, James A., ed. *Teaching Ethnic Studies.* Washington, D.C.: National Council for the Social Studies, 1973.

Banks, in editing this 43rd yearbook of the National Council for the Social Studies, has brought together a group of authors who present conceptual frameworks for studying about ethnic groups and analyzing American society. Institutional racism, social justice, and power relations are perceptively analyzed with suggestions given on how the teacher can effectively deal with individual and institutional racism. The book also deals with the problems of specific ethnic groups, focusing on historical and sociological experiences and how these can be incorporated into the social studies curriculum. The authors strongly admonish that educators and laymen must be able to view minority cultures from the points of view of the victims of oppression since prevailing conceptions of these groups have reflected an Anglo-Saxon bias.

Banks, James A., *Teaching Strategies for Ethnic Studies.* Boston, Mass.: Allyn and Bacon, Inc. 1975.

Banks is advocating the teaching of not only ethnic studies but of comparative ethnic studies as well. He presents content, strategies, concepts, and resources which are intended to serve as a guide for present and future teachers in teaching and integrating ethnic studies and content into the curriculum. The format of the book is such that the first half deals with those instructional problems that are basic to the teaching of ethnic studies, while the second half is devoted to different individual ethnic groups and offers exemplary strategies for teaching key concepts and generalizations with ethnic content. The book, as a whole, offers a sound beginning in teachers' reconceptualizing their views of America in order to fully understand the nature of American society and the role that ethnicity plays within it.

Boyer, James B. and Joe L. Boyer, eds. *Curriculum & Instruction After Desegregation: Form, Substance & Proposals.* Manhattan, Kansas: Ag. Press, 1975.

This book addresses itself to the changes that must occur in the curriculum and instruction in schools following desegregation. The editors make an important distinction between desegregation and integration. Desegregation occurs when there is a change in the physical arrangement of people so that separation on racial-ethnic bases no longer exists. Integration is far more encompassing and involves social acceptance of people as equals. They recognize that desegregation of schools precedes integration and that the curriculum and instruction utilized in the desegregated situation prepares for and assists final integration. According to Boyer and Boyer, desegregation of the curriculum involves teacher and administrator self-analysis, examination of school practices, and changes in instructional approaches. The selections in the book reflect these components. The selections range from discussions of general issues such as preserving individual dignity in desegregation to delineations of specifics such as how the music curriculum should be changed. Included throughout are questions for discussion and self-analysis.

Brislin, Richard W., Walter Lonner, and Robert M. Throndike. *Cross-Cultural Research Methods.* New York: John Wiley and Sons, 1973.

Although the authors are psychologists, and the book is written against this background, its usefulness for educators is without question. The purpose of the book is to provide a guide for conducting cross-cultural research, and this is applicable to all related fields. This is both a justification for cross-cultural research in terms of theory-building, as well as a methodological guide. The book is divided into two parts. The first part presents the substantive issues in cross-cultural research. This includes different types of cross-cultural research, problems in translation of survey or testing items, survey methods, design, and conducting of experiments, cross-cultural use of tests, etc. Part II deals with the more technical phase of research, the specific techniques of assessment and analysis of data. Specific testing instruments are analyzed and two clear, non-mathematical chapters on multi-variate techniques from a cross-cultural perspective are included. Throughout, the authors have included illustrations and explanations from very recent research in all related fields.

Brown, Dee. *Bury My Heart at Wounded Knee.* New York: Holt, Rineholt, and Winston, Inc., 1971.

The rape of everything that is Indian is that upon which Dee Brown has focused attention. *Bury My Heart at Wounded Knee* tells the other side of the story behind the white man-Indian relations. The story is told through a compelling dramatization of how "the West was lost"—lost to the greed, the ignorance, the malice, of the white man, which was displayed and made righteous under the lofty banner of manifest destiny. In taking the land the white man massacred entire tribes, brought to near extinction the source of livelihood of these tribes, and almost vanished a culture. Dee Brown traces this shock-filled history of the Indian and the white man as the latter pursues and hunts down the former, taking his land and destroying what he (the white man) does not want. The atrocities the white man commits against the Indian are only surpassed by the realization that the atrocities the Indian committed against the white man, he learned from the white man. Dee Brown's narrative is made even more dramatic because it is told in the words of the Indians: "They [white Americans] made us many promises, more than I can remember, but they never kept but one; they promised to take our land, and they took it."

Carter, Thomas P. *Mexican Americans in School: A History of Educational Neglect.* Princeton, New Jersey: College Entrance Examination Board, 1970.

Carter's study of the problems of schooling for Mexican Americans in the Southwest has resulted in a most comprehensive work on the role of education in the lives of Mexican Americans. In presenting the influence of the socioeconomic system the Mexican American lives in, Carter attempts to discourage the circular nature of arguments of why Mexican Americans do poorly in school: because they are poor, speak Spanish, and follow a traditional folk culture or vice versa. To obtain some of his data, Carter interviewed school people and laymen, focusing on six areas of concern: 1) the extent and nature of the experience of the interviewer with Mexican Americans; 2) a description of the ethnic and socioeconomic community served by the school; 3) the nature of the school in terms of organization, segregation, special programs, etc.; 4) the interviewer's perceptions of Mexican American children, their personalities, families, community; 5) achievement in school and years of schooling of local Mexican Americans contrasted with other groups; 6) reasons for Mexican Americans' success or failure in school. Some of the responses given Carter in the course of these interviews are enough to shake anybody's belief in school people and their work. There is no denying that the Mexican American suffers innumerable inequities and injustices in society and the educational system. In order to improve the performance of Mexican American schools Carter suggests, in his closing statements, three ways to accomplish this: change the student, change the school, or change society. Since the first one has not worked, is it not time we look for the answer elsewhere?

Della-Dora, Delmo and House, James E. eds. *Education for an Open Society.* Washington, D.C.: Association for Supervision and Curriculum Development, 1974.

60

This book seeks to go beyond the issue of ethnic differences in the schools. It addresses itself to the problem of creating an open society and the role played by educators in this task. The authors look forward to a society in which all people regardless of ethnicity, sex, culture, or lifestyle have a voice, a society in which such differences are not merely tolerated, but valued. The selections included examine the history and progress we have made in achieving an open society, the relationship between the school and society, and the specific aspects of the educational process which require reform—the curriculum, instructional media, teachers. The book then turns to a discussion of the concept of power in an open society, a theme that is central to the entire volume. It is a fundamental premise that in an open society power must be shared and shared willingly, and this concept must be put into operation in the educational system. The volume concludes with a discussion by the contributors concerning the part that educators can play in opening society. While optimistic in note, the authors are fully aware of the limitations of the schools. They point out that school is only one aspect of the total community, and thus must work together with the community if the objective is to be realized.

While addressing the theoretical concepts of freedom and power, the book—because of the nature of its contributors—offers a pragmatic consideration of the subject not often found in such discussions.

Dunfee, Maxine, ed. *Eliminating Ethnic Bias in Instructional Materials: Comment and Bibliography*. Washington, D.C.: Association for Supervision and Curriculum Development, 1974.

This booklet, which is a result of ASCD's Commission on Ethnic Bias in Preparation and Use of Instructional Materials begun in 1969, is primarily a bibliography to assist teachers in choosing and devising more appropriate materials for use in a multicultural society. There are over 300 items (some of which are also bibliographies) divided into four sections, each headed by a short justifying essay by a different contributor. The sections are entitled "A Rationale for a Pluralistic Society," "Evidence of Ethnic Bias in Instructional Materials," "Efforts to Change," and "Resources for Educators." A wide variety of resources concerned with many cultural groups are included. Also included is a guide for teacher-evaluation of textbook material.

Fishman, Joshua A. *A Sociology of Bilingual Education*. New York: Zeshiva University, 1974.

In this report, Fishman describes what bilingual education is not as well as what it is. He points out that the United States is of a Neanderthal mentality in believing that linguistic heterogeneity is related to economic disadvantage and/or ethnic diversity. He emphatically attempts to stress that bilingualism is a good thing for all children. His greatest effort is in his advocation of secondary bilingual education. He cites worldwide examples of secondary bilingual education, predicts respectable success of bilingual secondary education the world over. All the United States need do now is jump on the bandwagon.

Freire, Paulo. *Pedagogy of the Oppressed*. New York: Herder & Herder, 1971.

The Pedagogy of the Oppressed represents the first English publication of the work of Brazilian educator Paulo Freire. Freire views education as the process by which the oppressed become aware of themselves and their social reality and in the process liberate themselves. He defines a pedagogy in which the students and teacher together become critical investigators of the students' world. By decoding their world, the oppressed come to view their situation only as a limiting one which by their actions they can transform. In delineating his pedagogy, Freire discusses the nature of both the oppressor and the oppressed.

He repudiates the "banking" concept of education in which the teacher becomes the depositor and the student, the depository. His system includes problem posing investigation of themes, critical dialogue, and synthesis. The book is not meant to be a guide for implementation; it justifies the theoretical basis and outlines the approach. More importantly, it presents a thought-provoking definition of the educational process and the teacher/student relationship which can have important implications for the oppressed in this society as well.

Glazer, Nathan & Daniel P. Moynihan. *Beyond the Melting Pot*. Cambridge, Mass.: The M.I.T. Press, 1970.

Glazer and Moynihan have put together a quite perceptive inquiry into the dilemma of ethnic minorities with New York City providing the most uncommon of settings. They have given the main character role first to Blacks, because it is what strikes one as most obvious, and have proceeded from there looking backward at Puerto Ricans, Jews, Italians, and the Irish. The book is thus addressed to the role of ethnicity in the tumultuous variety that is New York City. It is addressed to the never-ending drama, played out in different colors which can never be eliminated or assimilated, of the stark reality that is New York. New York politics, New York economics, New York religion, New York employment, New York education—all of which have their avowed interest groups. The internal aspects of and between these issues, however, are complicated by the inescapable fact that in New York City as in no other place in the country, each interest group is synonymous to an ethnic group. This complexity can be smoothed out somewhat by general acceptance of the fact that all policies are inevitably policies for ethnic and race relations. The authors wisely point out that ethnicity in the United States is here to stay; it can no longer "melt." Ethnicity is the American nationality.

Glock, Charles E. et al. *Adolescent Prejudice*. New York: Harper & Row, 1975.

Glock and his co-authors have put together an excellent analysis of what accounts for adolescent prejudice as well as its absence. The authors' main focus is on anti-Semitism while at the same time contrasting it to racial prejudice. Their findings closely link deprivation with prejudice and indicate that the highest degree of prejudice is found among those who have not developed the cognitive skills and sophistication necessary to combat it.

62

Gollnick, Donna, Frank H. Klassen, Joost Yff. *Multicultural Education and Ethnic Studies in the United States: An Analysis Annotated Bibliography of Selected ERIC Documents.* Washington, D.C.: American Association of Colleges for Teacher Education and ERIC Clearinghouse on Teacher Education, 1976.

This publication represents a cooperative effort between AACTE's Ethnic Heritage Center and ERIC Clearinghouse on Teacher Education to provide a bibliography of multicultural materials available through ERIC. The fully annotated bibliography contains over 200 items, 20 of which are themselves bibliographies or directories. The materials are divided by section into concept materials, program materials, and other materials. Within these sections, the items are further divided by type or instructional level. The very complete annotations and the classification process employed renders the bibliography highly usable and useful. Also included are a literature review/rationalization for multiculture education, a detailed explanation of the selection and classification procedures and in the preparation of the bibliography, and information pertinent to the utilization of the ERIC system and materials pertaining to bilingual education although a similar bibliography for this area is anticipated.

Goodman, Mary Ellen. *The Culture of Childhood: Child's Eye-View of Society and Culture.* New York: Teachers College Press, 1970.

Utilizing studies of children from a variety of cultures—the Philippines, Japan, Puerto Rico, New Zealand, the Middle East, and middle class and minority America—Mary Ellen Goodman examines what it is that constitutes the child's eye-view of the world. She considers such aspects as awareness of self, others, and society, language, family relationships, responsibility, citizenship, values transmission, cognitive development, and play. Her thesis is twofold: 1) there are no universal age/stage linkages for development; and 2) parents and teachers underestimate what children even at a very young age are capable of perceiving and understanding. She postulates that children very early in life begin the process of absorbing the culture of the society around them; there is no universal culture of childhood other than that it reflects from society to society the culture of the adults. This book has implications for those educators who are in search of *the* correct method for educating children—all over the world and by a variety of methods children are becoming successful adults. There are also important implications for the field of multicultural education—assumptions cannot be made about universals even among the children from one country where there may be found many different cultural groups.

Grant, Carl, ed. *Sifting and Winnowing: An Exploration of the Relationship Between Multicultural Education and CBTE.* University of Wisconsin—Madison; Teacher Corp Associates, 1975.

This book addresses itself to the question of whether or not Competency Based Teacher Education programs can adequately prepare teachers to teach in a multicultural society. Specifically, contributors were asked to respond to two questions: 1) What is the role of their own or one particular component in education in assuring that CBTE includes multicultural education? and 2) What are the difficulties involved in relating multicultural education and CBTE? The diverse nature of articles includes perspectives on university teacher education curriculum, certification, evaluation of materials and community involvement. The overall response is that there is a logical and necessary relationship between multicultural education and CBTE. While most contributors caution against pitfalls, only the NEA presents a pessimistic view, stemming from its concern about the effectiveness of CBTE. Also included are the results of research by the editor assessing the progress of U.S. colleges in planning and implementing multicultural CBTE programs.

Grebler, Leo, Joan W. Moore, and Ralph C. Guzman. *The Mexican American People.* New York: The Free Press, 1970.

The authors have presented the most comprehensive study to date about the nation's second largest minority. The authors have analyzed the Mexican American as an ethnic minority and as a part of the American populace. As a result of research, questionnaires, and field work in Los Angeles and San Antonio the Mexican American is viewed from a historical, cultural, religious, and political perspective. The Mexican American's personal life is unfolded as the authors reveal fact and fiction about his role in the class structure, the family and in our changing social world. The conclusions drawn after a four-year study contradict many long-held popular and scholarly views of the Mexican American. Though extremely long, the book is well-written and the reader is provided with summaries at the end of each chapter which present in capsule form the overwhelming information, data, and statistics presented in each chapter.

Green, Robert L., ed. *Racial Crisis in American Education.* Chicago: Follet Educational Corporation, 1969.

This book examines the problem of minority education in America's schools, but because of the publication date, it lacks the broadened view that has emerged in the past few years. The primary concern is with Black students in the urban setting. Selections address themselves to such topics as the educational status of Blacks, the Relationship between Black Power and education, characteristics of the urban school child, teachers' attitudes toward minority children, textbooks, compensatory education, Black English, and community control of schools. As the editor states, the themes which predominate throughout the book are that minority children are capable of learning and that the public schools must discover the appropriate means for facilitating their learning.

Harrington, Michael. *The Other America.* New York: The MacMillan Company, 1962.

Michael Harrington has provided us with a startling portrait of the poor in America. He refers to them as "the other America," an America visible and all too real only to those who are living in a culture of poverty. This shocking report unfolds the struggling economics of the aged, the unskilled workers, and racial and ethnic minorities perpetuated and exacerbated by the affluency which has blinded the majority of Americans to the plight of the poor. This barrier, this wall of affluence, which keep the poor invisible, has proved to be too formidable an object for the inadequate anti-poverty programs put into force with inadequate funding by a government which has attempted only to take token measures towards the abolition of poverty. It was during his tenure in office that President Truman stated that 1/3 of the nation was ill-housed, ill-clothed, and ill-fed. Since then the United States has come to provide for its citizens the highest standard of living known to man. However, Truman's statement, made some 25 years ago, is still as valid as if it had been made yesterday, and even more so. Herein lies the paradox. The millions of Americans who enjoy the affluency made possible by a distorted economy cannot, will not, abolish poverty.

Hunter, William A., ed. *Multicultural Education Through Competency-Based Teacher Education*. Washington, D.C.: American Association of Colleges for Teacher Education, 1974.

Hunter has presented the reader with a series of essays which expound that the "goal of education in contemporary society must be to develop individuals who are open to change and who are flexible, adaptive, and receptive." The authors of the various essays are in agreement that this must be preceded by students being introduced to the "great diversity of lifestyles which our multicultural heritage embraces." The schools' objective from this respect would be to design and implement a culturally pluralistic curriculum which accurately represents our diverse society. This design and implementation will occur when two basic premises Hunter makes are met: 1) teachers need certain competencies accommodating cultural diversity to function in any situation; once these competencies have been identified, they must be incorporated into preservice and inservice programs; and 2) teachers need certain unique competencies in order to teach in culturally diverse situations. The book thus is designed in a format which focuses on competencies generalizable to the teaching of all groups and on competencies that can differ among groups.

Illich, Ivan. *Deschooling Society*. New York: Harper & Row, 1970.

Ivan Illich takes a look at education as it exists in this country and throughout the world and concludes that what is needed is the deinstitutionalization of the educational system and, indeed, of society itself. Illich proposes that modern society has produced institutionalization of values as a result of equating progress with production, and this can only lead to "pollution, social polarization, and psychological impotence." The whole of society requires disestablishment in order to avoid the consequences, but this book focuses primarily on the educational system. Education has become synonymous with schooling, a view that is not only economically unfeasible, but one which subverts the meaning of education. Illich presents his plan for the deinstitutionalization of schools—eliminating compulsory attendance, age requirement, specified curriculum, and discrimination in employment based on school attendance or certification, and replacing them with a system which would permit education to occur casually at the discretion of the learner. This would involve a system of easily accessible reference services, skill exchanges where individuals instruct others in skills they possess, and peer-matching where those with common interests can come together to discuss, share, and learn. School buildings would be returned to the community for the use of anyone who wished to share knowledge, and a new breed of professional educators would emerge to provide guidance and assistance. This is a provocative book for those of us considering ourselves professional educators.

Jencks, Christopher (et al). *Inequality: A Reassessment of the Effect of Family and Schooling in America*. New York: Harper & Row, 1972.

In this book, Christopher Jencks and his colleagues at the Center for Educational Policy Research at Harvard challenge some of our more fundamental assumptions concerning school reform. They conclude that educational reform cannot appreciably reduce the social and economic inequality that exists in this society. Any change in society must be addressed directly; change will not occur by employing the indirect and ineffective method of equalization of educational opportunity. Because the school cannot affect any long-term change in society, any reform should, therefore, be aimed at improving educational environment for both students and teachers.

The authors arrive at these conclusions by examining the inequality that exists in the schools, the inequality in cognitive skills and educational attainment of students, and analyzing the factors that are commonly felt to affect the inequality —school quality, resources, segregation, heredity, family background, curriculum. They then examine occupational and economic inequality and analyze the factors which are believed to affect these—educational attainment, race, cognitive skills, family background. They utilize a wide range of surveys for their data, but the authors readily admit that the data used is often weak and the conclusions far from definite. For this reason their conclusions are often based on trends rather than on any hard and fast proof. Nevertheless, the arguments are persuasive and certainly should be considered before any wholesale reform is to be undertaken.

Kallen, Horace M. *Culture and Democracy in the United States*. New York: Boni and Liveright, 1924.

". . . unless our education is nationalized in a way which recognizes that the peculiarity of our nationalism is its internationalism, we shall breed enmity and division in our frantic efforts to secure unity . . . ." Thus, with incredible insight Kallen predicted what has come to be and what will continue to be unless we realize and accept the pluralistic nature of our society. Throughout his book Kallen emphasizes the fact that America is what it is not by reason of what earlier immigrants found here but by what they brought with them. He cautions against conformity as the "appearance of security" thus feeding the delusion of safety. Kallen concludes that our chief virtue, for survival's sake, must be interracial tolerance.

66

Montague, Ashley. *Man's Most Dangerous Myth: The Fallacy of Race.* New York: Oxford University Press, 1974.

Originally published in 1942, this book remains a classic in the field of scientific investigation of race. Montague's purpose is to destroy with scientific evidence the myths on which racial prejudice are built. His central thesis is that the traditional concepts of race which have viewed various ethnic groups as having inborn combinations of physical, mental, and cultural traits which set them apart from other "races" are totally without foundation. In supporting this thesis, Montague examines the historical development of the concept of "race" and the roles of anthropologists, slavery, and society in the perpetuation of unfounded notions. He then analyzes the concepts in terms of scientific evidence, examining the role of biological, social, and psychological factors in creating ethnic differences. Separate chapters are devoted to discussions of myths surrounding the American Indian, American Negro, and Jew. Newly added chapters to this edition respond to Arthur Jensen's work and to the question of sociogenic brain damage. He concludes with a discussion of the devastating effects of racism on democracy and the role of educators in rooting out racism. The fifth edition is revised and the extensive bibliography updated to help maintain the status of the work as an important contribution to the study of ethnic differences.

Novak, Michael. *The Rise of the Unmeltable Ethnics.* New York: Macmillan Publishing Co., 1973.

The politics of the 60's was dominated by concern for Blacks and the 70's, according to Novak, will herald the rise of the forgotten, white, and unmelted ethnics—those whose origins are Southern and Eastern Europe, the Greeks, Italians, Poles, and Slavs. This book is a revelation of what it has meant to be a white ethnic in this country. It has meant facing two kinds of prejudice: the Nordic racism of the Northern Europeans and the intellectual prejudice of the "educated class." This is not a book of statistics; it is a book of personal feelings, attitudes, values, philosophies, dreams. In revealing the white ethnic, Novak exposes the "superculture" and its commitment to WASP values and the values of modernity. Three themes emerge throughout: 1) the unconscious hold of ethnic origins on people; 2) the decline of the hold of WASP values on the country as a whole and; 3) the more likely tolerance to be found among white ethnics. He calls for and predicts a new Ethnic Democratic Party, a coalition of ethnic white and Black which will stand for genuine cultural variety and people before technology.

Poblano, Ralph, ed. *Ghosts in the Barrio.* San Rafael, California: Leswing Press, 1973.

Poblano has put together a collection of essays focusing on what the Chicano has endured and what he must still endure in order to survive. The essays cover various aspects of the Chicano and his environment, including stereotypes and definitions, employment, the political process, bilingual-bicultural education, the training and retraining of teachers and instructional styles. Contributors include such well known Chicanos as Ernesto Galarza,

Tomas Arcienega, Mari-Luci Jaramillo, and Alfredo Castañeda. The book's central theme emphasizes that educators and society in general must recognize the Chicano not only as a person but a person with a history and a culture which today have so profoundly affected his status.

Ramirez, Manuel and Alfredo Castañeda. *Cultural Democracy, Bicognitive Development, and Education.* New York: Academic Press, 1974.

Ramirez and Castañeda have focused on cultural democracy, bicultural identity, and bicognitive development in the education of the Mexican American child. A culturally democratic learning environment, according to the authors, is a setting in which the Mexican American child can acquire knowledge about his own culture and the dominant culture. Bicultural identity refers to the ability to function competently in two cultures. Bicognitive development, the thesis of Ramirez' and Castañeda's book, suggests that culturally different children come to school with a different cognitive style than their Anglo counterparts and the authors' thesis enables them to develop both cognitive styles in culturally democratic educational environments.

In expounding their thesis, the authors discuss several things. The melting pot theory and its affect on culturally different children is discussed. They come out against compensatory education on the basis of its underlying assumption that something is wrong with the child and the child's culture and language interferes with his intellectual and emotional development. Ramirez and Castañeda discuss the composition of Mexican American culture and conclude that Mexican American children experience difficulty in school because their culture is not given recognition and school personnel, more often than not, are not aware of differences between traditional Mexican American and mainstream American middle class cultures. Much attention is focused on the concept of field sensitivity and field independence and how this can be used to explain the differences in performance of Mexican American and Anglo children on cognitive tasks. This concept is carried a step further in identifying Mexican American children in their extent of identification with traditional Mexican American values.

The ideas presented by Ramirez and Castañeda were long overdue. Their educational implications are tremendous. Pluralism must become synonymous with education. It is only through pluralistic education that we will be able to transform these educational implications into educational implementations.

Smith, Arthur. *Transracial Communication.* Englewood Cliffs, New Jersey: Prentice-Hall, Inc., 1973.

This book is an examination of race as a variable in oral communication. It goes beyond a discussion of cultural differences which may interfere with communication. Smith looks at the whole process of verbal communication between people, as the usual constraints and pressures that are operating in any communication when the initiators are of different racial backgrounds. He presents a model of transracial communication illustrating the operation of the process of "normalization" by which the initiators in transracial communication reach the stage where they can expose their genuine selves without affectation. The remainder of the book is devoted to an examination of those elements which affect the process of normalization—control beliefs, stereotyping, communication skills, perception, symbols, metacommunication, sex, and social stratification.

Steinfield, Melvin. *Cracks in the Melting Pot: Racism and Discrimination In American History.* New York: Glencoe Press, 1973.

The intent of this book is to expose the melting pot myth of American society, to show the extent to which racism has and still does exist. Because of an unusual format, the author is able to do this to an extent not usually possible. Each chapter includes a brief introduction by the author and a series of very short selections to illustrate the topic. These include passages from books and articles, news items, etc.—only the most germane portions are included. The opening section is concerned with putting America's racism in perspective by illustrating it as a worldwide problem. The book then proceeds to delineate how racism in America has been experienced by all minority groups, how racism has been used to rationalize territorial acquisition, how it has been manifested against particular immigrant groups, Chinese, Japanese, Jews and others, and how it has been manifested against Blacks, legally and extralegally. There is a particularly interesting chapter on Presidential racism from George Washington to Richard Nixon. The final chapters review events and attitudes of the 60's and 70's and conclude that the future is bleak, that racism has created deep wounds in society for both its majority and minority members which will be difficult to heal.

Stent, Madelon, D., William R. Hozard, Harry N. Rivlin. *Cultural Pluralism in Education: A Mandate for Change.* New York: Appleton-Century-Crofts, 1973.

The book is a result of TTTLTI's (Training the Teacher Trainers Leadership Training Institute) Conference on Education for Cultural Pluralism held in May, 1971. The book reflects the philosophy of the conference in several ways. First is the emphasis on action, a desire to have more to show than a published set of papers. Included are specific and feasible suggestions for implementing the philosophy of cultural pluralism in education. Reflected in the papers is the emphasis on cooperation between community, university, and school in the implementation of multicultural programs. Also reflected is the dedication to the principle of cultural pluralism itself. Papers were solicited pertaining to aspects of Asian, Puerto Rican, and American`Indian culture. The book provides a good overview of the direction in which multiculture education has been heading the past few years with an emphasis on the practical and feasible goals. Also included is a bibliography of films useful in multiculture education.

Stone, James C. and DeNevi, Donald P., eds. *Teaching Multi-cultural Populations: Five Heritages.* New York: Van Nostrand Reinhold Company, 1971.

This book is designed as an introductory text for the classroom teacher who needs a basic understanding of students from a different ethnic background. The title is somewhat misleading as only the introductory section addresses itself to the general question of teaching in a multicultural setting. The core of the book is devoted to acquainting the teacher with each of five ethnic groups: Blacks, Puerto Ricans, Mexican Americans, Indians, and Asian Americans. Because the book was published in 1971, the section on Asian Americans includes only Chinese and Japanese and does not concern itself with the Vietnamese and Cambodians which now comprise a large portion of the Asians in this country. Within each section, selections are included which present the historical and cultural background of the particular ethnic group, selections which present a more personal or contemporary view of the group, and selections which deal with the issues involved in the education of the group. There is a balance of selections designed to be purely informational, and "how to." In an effort to maintain this format, the editors have included some selections of questionable value, as there is admittedly a shortage of good material available for each of the ethnic groups presented. Also included in the book are the authors' model for teacher preparation and an extensive bibliography including available teaching materials.

Turner, Paul R., ed. *Bilingualism in the Southwest.* Tucson, Arizona: The University of Arizona Press, 1973.

The collected essays in this book focus on the two distinct language and cultural groups of the Southwest: the Indian and the Mexican American. More importantly they address the axiom that bilingualism is a tradition in the Southwest. The contributing authors speak to bilingual education and ask if its ultimate objective is assimilation or pluralism. They also make unique, interesting, and contradictory observations on language resources and development, and on cultural and linguistic interactions. The authors, representing a number of different disciplines, demonstrate the diversity of academic interest in the "phenomena" of bilingualism which has become a social reality "so complex that no one discipline with its limited perspective is adequate to the task" of studying it (bilingualism). The sole theme that seems to run through all the essays is recognizing a privileged individual as one who speaks more than one language and participates in more than one culture, thus being "liberated from the intellectual provincialism of a single culture."

A Better Chance to Learn: Bilingual Bicultural Education. Washington, D.C.: United States Commission on Civil Rights, Clearinghouse Publication No. 51, May, 1975.

As a result of the research done to compile this report, the Commission has concluded that "bilingual bicultural education is the program of instruction which currently offers the best vehicle for large numbers of language minority students who experience difficulty in our schools." The bases for this conclusion are spelled out and footnoted meticulously. The Commission provides a historical overview of language minorities and education. The Commission expounds on equal educational opportunity citing research and offering English-as-a-second-language and bilingual bicultural education as the vehicles to achieve this mean. Descriptions of bilingual bicultural programs are given along with the varying program structures which are dictated by local needs. The Commission also suggests methods of evaluation and assessment. In view of the Commission's aforementioned conclusion, it is hoped that educators move immediately to overcome the barriers to education facing language minority students.

Educational Leadership. "Human Relations Curriculum—Teaching Students to Care and Feel and Relate." October, 1974.

The theme for this issue of *Educational Leadership,* "human relations curriculum—teaching students how to care, feel, and relate," is aptly carried out by several contributing authors who see the need for enhancing human relationships through education. Emphasis was placed on ideas, methods, and insights useful in implementing opportunities for learning experiences that would foster the affective goals in education. Although not neglecting the cognitive aspects of education, it is brought to the readers' attention that such aspects greatly depend upon the affective dimensions of the educational relationship.

Educational Leadership. "Toward Cultural Pluralism." December, 1974.

This issue of the journal of the Association for Supervision and Curriculum Development is devoted to the theme of cultural pluralism, the central theme adopted by the organization itself. It contains a wide range of topics—philosophical bases, community involvement, the counselor's role, teacher attitudes, religious minorities, cognitive styles, and implementation considerations. There is an emphasis on practical considerations from the viewpoint of the organization. It includes such well known contributors as James A. Banks, Gwendolyn C. Baker, and Alfredo Castañeda.

Journal of Teacher Education. "Multicultural Education" Washington, D.C.: AACTE. Winter, 1973.

The thematic section of this issue emerges from the American Association of Colleges for Teacher Education's statement on multicultural education, "No One Model American," which was adopted in 1972 and which heads this issue. This issue is unique among recent journal issues devoted to multicultural education. It is not a "how to" for teachers or administrators. Rather it debates some of the underlying philosophical issues relating to multicultural education. It discusses some of the serious questions that the most devoted of multicultural education proponents must address themselves to if multicultural education is to become more than another educational fad. These are questions of goals, meaning, and basic attitudes.

Kappan. "The Imperatives of Ethnic Education." James Banks, ed. Phi Delta Kappa, 8th & Union, Bloomington, Indiana. January, 1972.

This edition of *Kappan* presented its readers some of the first articles which strongly advocated multicultural education. Throughout the edition the contributing authors resound the same note: a call for multicultural education through the public schools. The irony inherent in that is the schools for so long

71

served mainly to reinforce social class and racial stratification. Now they are looked upon as possibly the only institution which will instill values which accept cultural differences. The price for not following through with a multicultural education is too great: the possibility of "losing forever the opportunity to foster inquiring minds, humane values, and positive identities."

Social Science Quarterly. "The Chicano Experience in the United States." March, 1973.

This expanded issue seeks to fill the void in social science's contribution toward understanding the Chicano experience. There are twenty-two articles based on research in a variety of areas—social status, health, attitudes, political behavior, language patterns, education, economics, family patterns. The contributors are primarily sociologists, but contributions from the fields of psychology, political science, economics, and business are also included. The diversity in the issue, while preventing depth and continuity, points out the state of research in the area and serves to encourage further research.

The Georgetown Law Journal. "Equal Educational Opportunity." March, 1973.

This issue is devoted to a symposium on "Equal Eductional Opportunity." The seven contributions provide an in-depth look at various aspects of the problem in its legal framework. The issues discussed are integration vs. compensatory education, school finances, busing, bilingual bicultural education, and the role of the judiciary in education reform. Congressman Alfonso Bell (Cal.) and Senator Joseph Montoya (N. Mex.) are among the contributors. The issue provides insight into the legal bases for many of the important educational discussions. Also included are discussion of the legal implications of standardized testing and the educational amendments of 1972.

The National Elementary Principal. "Education for the Spanish Speaking." November, 1970.

This issue is devoted to the problems faced by the Spanish speaking child in U.S. schools. Within this issue there is a wide range of topics presented. These range from the philosophical basis to specifics of individual programs. There are articles on background, methods, teacher preparation, community involvement, curriculum, and attitudes. The issue also includes articles centering on problems of Puerto Rican and Cuban students. A section on the role of the federal government contains responses by three legislators: Walter F. Mondale, Henry B. Gonzalez, and Edward R. Roybal. In addition there are portions of taped interviews with authorities Thomas P. Carter, Julian Samora, and George I. Sanchez concerning changes that have taken place and the future direction of education for the Spanish speaking.

MINI-REVIEWS FOR SECOND EDITION

Abrahams, Roger D., and Rudolph C. Troke, eds. Language and Cultural
   Diversity in American Education, Englewood Cliffs: Prentice-
   Hall, Inc., 1972.

This collection of essays is concerned with analyzing and understanding
the life-styles of those who are linguistically and culturally different from the
mainstream middle-class. It pinpoints some of the preconceptions which have
hindered the development of effective teaching methods in the schools, discusses
some cultural aspects of which teachers need to be aware, presents some basic
facts regarding the nature of language which teachers need to know in order to
develop an adequate linguisitc orientation in the classroom, and demonstrates
the application of some of these ideas and procedures.

Banks, James, Teaching Strategies for Ethnic Studies, Boston: Ally and Bacon,
   Inc., 1979.

This book, in the second edition, is designed to make teachers
cognizant of the content, strategies, concepts, and resources needed to teach
comparative ethnic studies and to integrate ethnic content into the regular
curriculum. It is divided into three parts--the first presenting the rationale
for teaching comparative ethnic studies; the second consisting of chapters on
the major American ethnic groups including a historical overview of each,
key concepts and teaching strategies, and annotated bibliographies for teachers
and students; and the third highlighting and summarizing the major points of
the previous chapters and illustrating how the teacher can use the information
and strategies to develop multiethnic units and curricula which focus on two
or more ethnic groups.

Carter, Thomas P. and Roberto D. Segura, Mexican Americans in Schools: A Decade of Change, Princeton: College Entrance Examination Board, 1979.

In the intervening ten years since the publication of Mexican Americans in School: A History of Educational Neglect through federal and state funding bilingual bicultural education and remedial and compensatory programs have been established. This book not only describes the problems but examines the proposed solutions. The past is contrasted with the present to answer such questions as--What changes have taken place? Has the social and academic achievement of the group significantly improved? If so, to what extent can this change be attributed to the efforts of the school? Which programs will most aid the Mexican American?

Cross, Dolores E. et al. eds. Teaching in a Multicultural Society: Perspectives and Professional Strategies, New York: The Free Press, 1977.

The basic purpose of this book is to advance the multicultural society by helping teachers and administrators to respond to prevailing multicultural conditions. This is accomplished through 1) the establishment of a historical framework for multicultural education and discussion of school and teacher attitudes, 2) awareness of the myths and realities of minority education and children, and 3) the discussion of programs and teaching strategies for a multicultural society.

Gold, Milton J. et al. eds. In Praise of Diversity: A Resource Book for Multicultural Education, Washington, D.C.: Teacher Corps-Association of Teacher Educators, 1977.

This book addresses itself to providing specific information about America's pluralism and professional skills and material to advance multicultural education. The introductory chapters deal briefly with basic considerations--

74

the pitfalls of stereotyping, pressure points, i.e. areas of likely conflict and controversy, and the implications for education. The section on ethnic vignettes which describes nine major ethnic or racial groups was designed to 1) develop an understanding of the cultural contributions of each group, 2) present the problems which minority groups have encountered and with which they still are confronted, 3) sketch the lifestyles and learning styles in different cultures so that teachers may more effectively work with them.

Grant, Carl A., ed. Multicultural Education: Commitments, Issues and Applications, Washington, D.C.: Association for Supervision and Curriculum Development, 1977.

This collection of articles was prepared as a resource for curriculum workers, teachers, and administrators. It provides various perspectives on multicultural education and discusses the specifics of curriculum design, multicultural materials and instructional activities, including suggestions for multicultural activities for the classroom.

Hansen-Krening, Nancy, Competency and Creativity in Language Arts: A Multi-ethnic Focus, Reading, Mass. Addison-Wesley Publishing Co., 1979.

This book was prepared as a resource text for using multiethnic materials in teaching basic language art skills. Each chapter provides the rationale for both the concept presented and its practical application. The practical applications consist of model lessons that utilize sensory awareness, music, art, drama, movement and literature to stimulate the development of basic skills in listening, verbal and nonverbal communication and writing.

Klassen, Frank H. and Donna M. Gollnick, eds. Pluralism and The American Teacher: Issues and Case Studies, Washington, D.C.: American Association of Colleges for Teacher Education, 1977.

Recognizing a need, AACTE compiled this collection of papers and reports to provide a better understanding of multicultural education for teachers and

75

its problems. Part I focusing on theoretical aspects, discusses the major necessary components, curriculum, the relationship between multicultural education and P/CBTE, and research. Part II, addressing practical aspects, consists of actual case studies of program development and programs at several major universities.

Krug, Mark, The Melting of the Ethnics, Bloomington: Phi Delta Kappa, 1976.

This book addresses itself to the evolution of the schools of thought concerning immigrants to the United States, namely the concept of the melting pot, Americanization and cultural pluralism. As examples three major immigrant groups, the Italians, Polish and Jews are discussed with respect to their history, immigration, and ethnic loyalties and affiliations. The two concluding chapters describe the educational experiences of the immigrants and the role the public schools played.

Mackey, William F. and Theodore Andersson, eds. Bilingualism In Early Child-
    hood, Rowley Mass.: Newbury House Publishers, 1977.

The proceedings of the Conference on Child Language, held in Chicago, in 1971, deal with two fields of inquiry--child language and bilingualism-- and reflect concern with the problems of ethnic minorities. Therefore, the papers range from the theoretical nature of language learning to case studies of individual preschool children of various ethnic groups. Still others discuss preschool programs, the primary curriculum and studies of bilingual programs. The last section deals with the questions of future research and the future of the ethnic languages. When the ethnic minorities become fluent in English, will their languages disappear or endure?

National Council for the Social Studies, Curriculum Guidelines for Multiethnic Education, Arlington, 1976.

With the disagreement that exists in the definition of multiethnic education by the schools, NCSS has prepared this set of guidelines to clarify issues and help schools design and implement effective programs. These Guidelines are divided into three sections--the first being the rationale and including a description of the new society, the nature of the school and learner, and a delineation of goals for school reform; the second being the actual guidelines, describing the ideal characteristics of school environments; and the third being a program evaluation checklist to assess school environments to determine to what extent they reflect the ideal characteristics of the Guidelines.

Spolsky, Bernard, ed. The Language Education of Minority Children. Rowley, Mass.: Newbury House Publishers, Inc., 1972.

Cognizant of the importance of language in the classroom and the need for schools to address themselves to the language problems of minority children, Bernard Spolsky has compiled this collection of papers dealing with contemporary concerns. Section one provides insight into the scope of the problem and a picture of the complexity of the sociolinguistic systems. Section two focuses on bilingualism and bilingual education, i.e. the reasons for teaching children in their native language, the relationship between bilingualism and thought and a discussion of various models. Section three deals with specific curricular issues, including teaching English as a second language, standard English to Black children and reading, and with language testing.

Thompson, Thomas, ed. The Schooling of Native America, Washington, D.C.:
American Association of Colleges for Teacher Education, 1978.

These essays, prepared by Native Americans who are intimately involved
in Indian education, are an outgrowth of the Native American Teacher Corps
Conference, held in 1973. They expound on the author's varied experiences and
discuss the problems and challenges of Indian education, from the need for
political mobilization to the planning and administration their schools and the
programs of Native American studies. They demonstrate the intense feeling and
commitment of the authors to this present movement to wrest control of their
social, economic and political institutions from non-Indians.

Wolf-Wasserman, Miriam and Linda Hutchinson, eds. Teaching Human Dignity:
Social Change Lessons for Every Teacher, Minneapolis, Minnesota:
Education Exploration Center, 1978.

This book is a compilation of experiences and lessons through which
the authors provide curriculum materials, process ideas, and available resources
and resource centers. These materials cover a wide range of topics, usually
regarded as areas of social change and/or personal conflict; e.g. labor,
racism, third world people and women, drugs, crime and imprisonment, death
and dying, and others.

GLOSSARY OF SELECTED TERMS
IN MULTICULTURAL EDUCATION

Glossary of Selected Terms in Multicultural Education*

1. **Desegregation**—Desegregation is a physical arrangement whereby persons of different racial-ethnic backgrounds work, learn, and live in the same setting. It is the legal reversal of a historical-economic-social practice of separating groups of individuals from each other on the basis of identifiable characteristics such as race or ethnic identity. In another context, it is the abolition of racial separation in public schools, facilities, and other institutions. Desegregation frequently occurs under coercion by court order or administrative-executive orders. In America, it is also thought of as a reversal of the "separate but equal" doctrine which was a basis for the assignment of pupils to public schools for many years.

2. **Integration**—Integration is a broader concept than desegregation, in that it involves the *social acceptance as equals* of persons who are racially-ethnically different. Integration involves the social process of accepting and respecting the rights of individuals, regardless of race, and it is a process which takes a much longer period of time than that of desegregation. Desegregation generally must precede integration. Integration cannot be as easily quantified as can desegregation.

3. **Segregation**—Segregation is the separation of an entity or group of individuals based on some identifiable characteristic which is frequently physical. Racial segregation was the separation of people on the basis of their racial identification. Racial minorities in the United States (under segregation) were restricted in their activities and environment due to the separation which was both geographic and psychological. In many instances, segregation is separation based on religious and socioeconomic factors.

4. **Ethnic Group**—An ethnic group is a group of people with a common heritage, such as a geographic heritage (Poles, Swedes, Italians), which can be distinguished due to cultural and sociological traits. All groups have both a racial identification and an ethnic identification. Black Americans, for example, are generally members of the Negroid race with African ethnicity. Mexican Americans are generally members of the Caucasian race with Mexican ethnicity, part of which is the Spanish language. Ethnicity may also be defined to include factors such as religion, language, folklore, and group activity.

5. **Racial Group**—A racial group is a division of mankind possessing traits that are transmissible by descent and sufficient to characterize it as a distinct human type. A racial group actually includes a complex distinction of degrees of human traits that are physical, linguistic, cultural, and psychological. The social dimensions of a racial group are usually the result of economic patterns and opportunities—with all the accompanying political

*Modified from *Curriculum and Instruction After Desegregation: Form, Substance, and Proposals*, James B. Boyer and Joe L. Boyer, eds. Ag Press, 1975.

influences. For many, skin color is the most distinguishing factor of racial identification. Although there are many racial groups, the three main anthropological identifications are: Negroid, Mongoloid, and Caucasoid.

6. **Ethnicity**—Ethnicity is the awareness of the uniqueness of one's ethnic identity by the individual members of the group. Such awareness also reflects itself in the pride which one takes in his-her ethnic identity. It also involves the potency of the identity expressed by members of that group, and these expressions are transmitted through the culture.

7. **Ethnocentricism**—Ethnocentricism is the state of having race or ethnic group as a central interest based on the attitude that one's own racial or ethnic group is superior to all others.

8. **Ethnology**—Ethnology is a science that deals with the division of mankind into races and their origin, distribution, relations, and characteristics.

9. **Stereotype**—A standardized mental picture that is held in common by many members of one group about another—and that represents an oversimplified opinion, affective attitude, or uncritical judgment. It is a preconceived or pre-judged idea about a group of people with diverse membership. While there are positive stereotypes, the most frequent reference is to those reflecting undesirable characteristics. While this concept usually has ethnic or racial connotations, stereotypes could also refer to other characteristics, such as "bookworm," "egghead," etc.

10. **Dejure Segregation**—Separation of races enforced by law; the separation of people in social-political-educational contexts according to accepted "law of the enforcing group." Dejure segregation usually refers to separation by law.

11. **Defacto Segregation**—Separation of races which is not the result of law, but the result of common practice and prevailing circumstances such as poverty and neighborhood composition. It is reflected in school enrollment when attendance assignment is made on the basis of "neighborhood school" concepts. Such separation is frequently based on social and economic factors.

12. **Racism**—Racism is the belief that race is the primary determinant of human traits and capacities and that racial differences produce the inherent superiority or inferiority of a particular race. Racism also involves the operation of those institutions which directly affect the lives of people and the philosophies on which their operations are based.

13. **Sexism**—Sexism is the belief that one sex (male or female) is inherently superior to the other. Such belief manifests itself in behaviors which restrict one sex from opportunities, activities, and privileges normally granted to the other sex. Sexism is also demonstrated in the behavior of persons and institutions which directly affect the lives of human beings. In recent times, this term has referred to discriminatory behavior against females.

14. **Elitism**—Elitism is the idea that one group (usually an economic group) is better than another based on the value judgments of that group regarding their attributes and characteristics. Elitism involves the concept of social

superiority because of economic advancement. Further, it incorporates the idea that one group in society is better able to govern and, therefore, should hold the political power. Elitism, however, may be practiced on several economic levels and may reflect a number of contributing factors.

15. **American Indian**—An individual whose ancestors were native inhabitants of the territory known as the United States. There are several tribes of these people whose ancestors were the original occupants of America. Europeans who met these inhabitants upon arrival thought they were on the subcontinent of India or the East Indies. American Indians are sometimes referred to as *Native Americans*.

16. **Black American**—An individual who is a member of the Negroid race (especially the African branch) distinguished from members of other races by physical features. These physical features do not include factors such as language and mental capabilities. Further, the identification as a Black American includes a racial pride which emphasizes sociological and psychological strengths gained as a result of "self-system examinations" in recent times. Identification as a Black American frequently rejects identification as a Negro—and this rejection is based on specific philosophical differences constituting ethnicity.

   For years, Americans of Negroid descent preferred to be identified as Negroes. This was an anthropological substitution to describe persons of black skin. Because many people perceived black color in negative terms, Negro was an accepted substitution. With the onset of desegregation, there is decreased rejection of black identity and preference for the use of the term *black* rather than *Negro*. The use of the term *Negro* frequently denoted a rejection of self while *Black American* identification is total acceptance of self including one's ethnic heritage.

   Afro-American is synonymous with Black American. The term further emphasizes the African ethnic identity.

17. **Mexican American**—The generic term used to describe an individual in America whose ancestors or parents came from Mexico or Spain. The term encompasses the broad spectrum of a diverse ethnic group, the largest bilingual (Spanish-English) ethnic group in the country. There are at least three sub-groups among Mexican Americans. The *Hispano* is an individual whose ancestors were the original colonizers in the Southwest Juan Onate and other Spanish colonists first settled the Rio Grande Valley of the Southwest during the 16th century; these Hispanos represented a cultural identification with Spanish traditions and customs. The *Mejicano* is an individual whose ancestors remained in or migrated to the Southwest after the Mexican American War and retained a cultural identification with Mexican traditions and customs, which consist of both *Indo* (Mexican Indian) and Spanish influences. The *Migrant* is an individual, either Hispano or Mejicano, who earns his living in the agricultural fields of this country. The Mexican American migrant stream begins in the Southwest (Southern Texas, New Mexico, Arizona, California) and goes north to Kansas through the Midwest to Michigan or north up the West Coast and the Imperial Valley of California.

   The obvious indicant of the Mexican American is his bilingualism. He speaks American English and a dialect of Spanish, a *calo*, which combines

Castilian, Mexican, and some English language forms. Ethnocentric labels for the *calo* have been "Tex-Mex" or "pocho," but in recent years linguists and anthropologists have recognized the *calo* as a rich, complex, rule-governed dialect indigenous to this country. The vitality of the *calo* also indicates the vitality of the Mexican American culture.

Chicano is a term that describes a person who is Mexican American as well as a philosophic orientation. The term traces its derivation back to the last part of the word *Mejicano* as pronounced by the Aztecs—*Meshicano*. From the ending of *Meshicano* comes "shicano" or "chicano." *Chicano* is an ingroup term used to show unity and nationalism among its members, and was at first associated with the militant or low economic Mexican segment, but it is gaining acceptance among various elements of the total Mexican American group as well as the Anglo society.

18. **Latin Americans or Latinos**—These are terms that describe groups who identify more with their New World roots than their Spanish origin. Among these are Cuban Americans, Puerto Rican Americans, and other Americans whose ancestors migrated to the United States from Latin America.

19. **Puerto Rican**—An individual whose ancestors came from the island called Boriquen that was later named Puerto Rico. The Taino Indians lived on the island, but Spaniards and Africans settled there and began families. Today, a Puerto Rican may have either Indian, African, or Spanish ancestry, or combinations of these. Because (at a later time) the French, Italian, and Irish also migrated to the island, Puerto Ricans of today may reflect part of that ancestry as well.

20. **Bilingual Education**—Bilingual education is the offering of formal and informal instruction in two languages—one of which is the native language of the predominant ethnic group undergoing instruction. Both languages are emphasized equally, and learners are encouraged to speak and write in both languages. The positive contribution of bilingual education is that learners develop the skill of expressing themselves in two languages rather than one. Most important, students are instructed in the language or vernacular most familiar to them. Bilingual education, therefore, is not foreign language instruction in two languages; it is instruction in the language of the student as well as instruction about the official language of the country. Countries such as Mexico, Canada, India, and the USSR have traditionally used the bilingual format in their public schools.

21. **Bicultural Education**—Bicultural education is the offering of formal and informal instruction in which emphasis is placed on the cultural variations represented in American society. Students are helped to enhance their pride in their varied cultural heritages and are permitted to exhibit these variations without penalty in curricular functions. Bicultural education also supports the philosophy that such a practice results in greater respect for all cultural variations. Bicultural education will eventually become multicultural education, which will pervade the school curriculum with cultural experiences that reflect the ethnic diversity of this country.

22. **Minority Studies**—Minority Studies are sets of content (or programs) which attempt to include study about non-white persons in America through a

composite approach. The concept embodies an attempt to teach content about all racial-ethnic minorities in the same program. The public school and college curriculum excluded such content for such a long time that such programs were established to rectify the omission. Minority Studies programs tend to emphasize the cultural and historical aspects of racial and ethnic minorities.

23. **Multi-Ethnic Studies**—Multi-Ethnic Studies are those instructional programs which attempt to give equal attention to content drawn from the *historical* and sociological heritage of various ethnic groups. Generally, the programs reflect ethnic groups represented in a given locality with an effort to give equal attention to those groups. The basic intent of Multi-Ethnic Studies, however, is to fill the instructional void created by curricular exclusion of ethnic minorities.

24. **Multi-Cultural Studies**—The anthropological concept of culture is extremely broad and includes the physiological, psychological, sociological dimensions of a group of people. The term Multi-Cultural Studies is basically synonymous with Multi-Ethnic Studies. They are those instructional sequences which attempt to reflect the totality of American culture, not through assimilation, but through acculturation and the visible distinction of one cultural variation from another. Multi-Cultural Studies address themselves to both the similarities and differences among people within the framework of equal respect for these traits. This idea is particularly significant in efforts to desegregate the American instructional program.

25. **Cultural Pluralism**—Cultural pluralism is the social, economic, and political variation in a given society and the anthropological patterns accompanying the variation. In terms of schools and the learning-teaching process, it means the recognition of variation through instructional approaches, materials, and assessment. It is not in conflict with multi-ethnic ideas and ideals, and it suggests the autonomous freedom of cultural variation among entities in the American milieu. Note: There are many variations of the definition of cultural pluralism other than the one above. Some definitions become more philosophical than is intended for this glossary.

26. **Separatism**—Separatism is a philosophical concept denoting the desire to be apart from another. Related to desegregation, it is the political-economic movement or ideology which proposes the separation of groups on the basis of racial or ethnic identity. Racial and ethnic minorities (numerical minorities in the United States) who choose to function apart from the racial and ethnic majority often hold the viewpoint that their interests can best be served through maintenance of self-government for that group. This philosophical position is frequently held among groups who have lost faith in the operational productivity of a "united" existence which excluded them or discriminated against them.

27. **Assimilation**—Assimilation, in many ways, is philosophically synonymous with the melting pot theory. It presupposes that all persons would like a common perception, a common curriculum, a common set of practices on which lives are based. Professional educators who lived by this philosophical base often provided a failure experience for those learners who did not

assimilate, either because of linguistic difference or economic disability, but particularly because of racial or ethnic identification.

28. **Acculturation**—Basically, acculturation is the process by which a human being acquires the culture of his society. Related to desegregation, it is the interchange or process or intercultural borrowing between diverse peoples resulting in new and blended patterns of living, learning, assessing.

29. **Afro-American Studies, Indian Studies, Chicano Studies, etc.**—These are curricular and instructional efforts to emphasize, through in-depth academic effort, the ancestry, contributions, and economic, political, social, and religious identities of a particular racial or ethnic group. Afro-American Studies, for example, are concerned with the history and the sociological, humanistic, and technological data of those Americans with African ancestry (who generally happen to be of Negroid descent). Such programs of study have attempted to fill the void in public school curriculum which has traditionally omitted such content. Indian Studies, Chicano Studies, and Puerto Rican Studies serve the same basic purpose for other racial-ethnic minorities.

30. **Curriculum Bias**—Curriculum bias is inherent favoritism toward one economic or racial group over another. Such bias is usually reflected in textbooks, other instructional materials, standardized tests, and various artifacts which constitute the substance of school curriculum in America. The bias exists when those groups who are not substantively reflected in school programs are called on to respond as though they were. It should be remembered that the curriculum is composed primarily of the substance of learning and that the form of that learning involves us with instructional proficiency.

31. **Instructional Discrimination**—Instructional discrimination is the pedagogical act, practice, or behavior that results in unfair or inappropriate response to the varied learning styles of students. Further, it is any assumption that all persons learn most effectively from listening to the teacher. Equal instructional opportunity or equal learning opportunity results when varied teaching approaches are employed so that varied learning styles may receive an appropriate reaction or response.

32. **Desegregation Barrier**—A desegregation barrier is any physical, financial, political, philosophical, or psychological deterrent to the level of interracial schooling which fosters genuine, authentic respect for racial and ethnic differences. One such barrier is the lack of opportunity for individuals to "unlearn prejudices" and to examine discriminatory behavior.

BIBLIOGRAPHY--SELECTED WORKS

Andersson, Theodore and Mildred Boyer. Bilingual Schooling in the United
States. 2 vols. Austin, Texas: Southwest Educational Development
Laboratory, 1970.

Banks, James A. and Jean D. Grambs, eds. Black Self-Concept. New York:
McGraw-Hill Book Co., 1972.

Banks, James A., ed. Teaching Ethnic Studies. Washington, D.C.: National
Council for the Social Studies, 1973.

Banks, James A. Teaching Strategies for Ethnic Studies. Boston, Mass.: Allyn
and Bacon, Inc., 1975.

Banks, James A. Teaching Strategies for Ethnic Studies, Boston, Mass.: Allyn
and Bacon, Inc. 2nd edition, 1979.

Boyer, James B. and Joe L. Boyer, eds. Curriculum & Instruction After Desegregation:
Form, Substance & Proposals. Manhattan, Kansas: Ag. Press, 1975.

Brislin, Richard W., Walter Lonner, and Robert M. Throndike. Cross-Cultural
Research Methods. New York: John Wiley and Sons, 1973.

Brown, Dee. Bury My Heart at Wounded Knee. New York: Holt, Rineholt, and Winston,
Inc., 1971.

Carter, Thomas P. Mexican Americans in School: A History of Educational Neglect.
Princeton, New Jersey: College Entrance Examination Board, 1970.

Carter, Thomas P. and Roberta D. Segura, Mexican Americans in School: A Decade
Of Change, New York: College Entrance Examination Board, 1979.

Cross, Delores et al. eds., Teaching in a Multicultural Society: Perspectives and
Professional Strategies, New York: The Free Press, 1977.

Della-Dora, Delmo and House, James E., eds. Education for an Open Society.
Washington, D.C.: Association for Supervision and Curriculum Development, 1974.

Dunfee, Maxine, ed. Eliminating Ethnic Bias in Instruction Materials: Comment
and Bibliography. Washington, D.C.: Association for Supervision and Curriculum
Development, 1974.

Epps, Edgar, ed. Cultural Pluralism. McCutchan Co., 1974.

Fishman, Joshua A. A Sociology of Bilingual Education. New York Zeshiva University,
1974.

Freire, Paulo. Pedagogy of the Oppressed. New York: Herder & Herder, 1971.

Glazer, Nathan & Daniel P. Moynihan. Beyond the Melting Pot. Cambridge, Mass.:
The M.I.T. Press, 1970.

Glock, Charles E., et al. Adolescent Prejudice. New York: Harper & Row, 1975.

Gold, Milton J. et al. eds., In Praise of Diversity: A Resource Book for Multicultural Education, Washington, D.C.: Teacher Corps, 1977.

Gollnick, Donna, Frank H. Klassen, Joost Yff. Multicultural Education and Ethnic Studies in the United States: An Analysis Annotated Bibliography of Selected ERIC Documents. Washington, D.C.: American Association of Colleges for Teacher Education and ERIC Clearinghouse on Teacher Education, 1976.

Goodman, Mary Ellen. The Culture of Childhood: Child's Eye-View of Society and Culture. New York: Teachers' College Press, 1970.

Goodman, Mary Ellen. Race Awareness in Young Children. Collier Books, 1964.

Grant, Carl A., ed. Multicultural Education: Commitments, Issues, and Applications, Washington, D.C.: Association for Supervision and Curriculum Development, 1977.

Grant, Carl, ed. Sifting and Winnowing: An Exploration of the Relationship Between Multi-Cultural Education and CBTE. Teacher Corps Associates, University of Wisconsin-Madison, 1975.

Grebler, Leo, Joan W. Moore, and Raph C. Guzman. The Mexican American People. New York: The Free Press, 1970.

Green, Robert L., ed. Racial Crisis in American Education. Chicago: Follet Educational Corporation, 1969.

Haley, Alex. Roots. Garden City: New York, Doubleday & Company, 1976.

Harrington, Michael. The Other America. New York: The MacMillan Company, 1962.

Hunter, William A., ed. Multicultural Education Through Competency-Based Teacher Education. Washington, D.C.: American Association of Colleges for Teacher Education, 1974.

Illich, Ivan. Deschooling Society. New York: Harper & Row, 1970.

Jencks, Christopher, et al. Inequality: A Reassessment of the Effect of Family and Schooling in America. New York: Harper & Row, 1972.

Kallen, Horace M. Culture and Democracy in the United States. New York: Boni and Liveright, 1924.

Klassen, Frank H. and Donna Gollnick, eds., Pluralism and the American Teacher: Issues and Case Studies, Washington, D.C.: American Association of Colleges for Teacher Education, 1977.

Kloss, Heinz. The American Bilingual Tradition. Rowley, Mass.: Newbury House Publishers, 1977.

Krening, Nancy Hansen. Competency and Creativity in Language Arts: A Multiethnic Focus. Reading, Mass.: Addison-Wesley Publishing Co., 1979.

Krug, Mark. The Melting of the Ethnics. Bloomington, Indiana: Phi Delta Kappa, 1976.

Ladner, Joyce, ed. The Death of White Society, Vintage Books, 1973.

Lambert, W. E. and G. R. Tucker. Bilingual Education of Children. Newbury House Publisher, 1972.

Mackey, William F. and Theodore Andersson, editors, Bilingualism in Early Childhood. Rowley, Mass.: Newbury House Publishers, 1977.

Montague, Ashley. Man's Most Dangerous Myth: The Fallacy of Race. New York: Oxford University Press, 1974.

Mydral, Gunnar. An American Dilemma. Vols. I & II, Harper & Row 1944, 1962.

Novak, Michael. The Rise of the Unmeltable Ethnics. New York: MacMillan Publishing Co., 1973.

Poblano, Ralph, ed. Ghosts in the Barrio. San Rafael, California: Leswing Press, 1973.

Ramirez, Manuel and Alfredo Castaneda. Cultural Democracy, Bicognitive, Development, and Education. New York: Academic Press, 1974.

Rose, Arnold. The Negro in America. Harper & Row, 1976.

Smith, Arthur. Transracial Communication. Englewoods Cliffs, New Jersey: Prentice Hall, 1973.

Spolsky, Bernard, ed., The Language of Minority Children. Rowley, Mass.: Newbury House Publishers, Inc., 1972.

Steinfield, Melvin. Cracks in the Melting Pot: Racism and Discrimination in American History. New York: Glencoe Press, 1973.

Stent, Madelon D., William R. Hozard, Harry N. Rivlin. Cultural Pluralism in Education: A Mandate for Change. New York: Appleton - Century-Crofts, 1973.

Stone, James C. and DeNevi, Donald P., ed. Teaching Multi-Cultural Populations: Five Heritages. New York: Van Nostrand Reinhold Company, 1971.

Thompson, Thomas, ed., The Schooling of Native America. Washington, D.C.: American Association of Colleges for Teacher Education, 1978.

Turner, Paul R., ed. Bilingualism in the Southwest. Tucson, Arizona: The University of Arizona Press, 1973.

Valverde, Leonard A., ed., Bilingual Education for Latinos. Washintgon, D.C.: Association for Supervision and Curriculum Development, 1978.

Walker, Judith. Education in Two Languages: A Guide for Bilingual Teachers. Washington, D.C.: University Press of America, 1979.

JOURNALS AND PAMPHLETS

A Better Chance to Learn: Bilingual Bicultural Education. Washington, D.C.:
United States Commission on Civil Rights, Clearinghouse Publication No. 51,
May, 1975.

Curriculum Guidelines for Multiethnic Education, National Council for the Social
Studies, Arlington, Virginia, 1976.

Educational Leadership. "Curriculum for Economic and Ethnic Diversity."
Washington, D.C.: ASCD, April, 1974.

Educational Leadership. "Human Relations Curriculum--Teaching Students to Care
and Feel and Relate." October, 1974.

Educational Leadership. "Multicultural Curriculum: Issues, Designs, Strategies."
December, 1975.

Educational Leadership. "Toward Cultural Pluralism." December, 1974.

Educational Perspectives, "Selected Aspects of Multicultural Education."
December, 1977.

Journal of Teacher Education. "Multicultural Education." Washington, D.C.:
AACTE. Winter, 1973.

Kappan. "The Imperatives of Ethnic Education." James Banks, ed. Phi Delta
Kappa, 8th & Union, Bloomington, Indiana. January, 1972.

Social Science Quarterly. "The Chicano Experience in the United States." March, 1973.

The Georgetown Law Journal. "Equal Educational Opportunity." March, 1973.

The National Elementary Principal. "Education for the Spanish Speaking." November,
1970.